ANTHROPOLOGY OF AGING : CONTEXTS, CULTURE AND IMPLICATIONS

ANTHROPOLOGY OF AGING : CONTEXTS, CULTURE AND IMPLICATIONS

Anand Akundy

SERIALS PUBLICATIONS
New Delhi

First Published -2021

ISBN 81-86771-52-2

Published by

Head Office : **SERIALS PUBLICATIONS**
4, B.S.S. Hall, Khyber Pass Market,
Civil Lines, Delhi–110054 (India)
Phone: 23245225
Fax: 91-11-23272135
e-mail: serials@satyam.net.in

Branch Office : *4830/24, Prahlad Street, Ansari Road,*
Darya Ganj, New Delhi-110002 (India)

Printed at :

PRINTED IN INDIA

Preface

This book entitled "Anthropology of aging: The context of retirement in a South Indian town" is a revised version of my Ph.D thesis and is based upon firsthand information collected from 200 retirees in Tirupati, Andhra Pradesh of whom 100 are gazetted and 100 are non-gazetted.

The data were obtained mainly with the help of a schedule and it was supplemented by interviews, observation, case studies, and informal discussions. The data were tabulated into two-way frequency tables for which Chi-square and `t' tests were conducted.

Research so far conducted on aged people in India and all over the world were reviewed and the relevant information was collected. In this context a lot of library work had to be done. This thesis is thus a result of months reading, field-work and writing about retired employees of Tirupati.

The present study is organized into ten chapters. Chapter-1 is introductory. It deals with the orientations and limitations of the study. Chapter-2 surveys the available literature on retirees with special reference to pre-retirement conditions, post-retirement changes and problems of retirees besides approaches to the study of retirees. It discloses how research on aging and the aged is still in its infancy in India and shows how the present inquiry is a modest attempt to add some more information to the existing investigations with reference to the aged people in an urban center in India. Chapter-3 depicts the methodology adopted for studying the sample respondents. Chapter-4 focusses it attention on the background of the urban place where the retirees are residing. Chapters-5 to 9 present work and retirement of the employees, economic and familial adjustment of the retirees, and the socio-psychological and the health problems of the retirees. Chapter-10 summarizes the study and gives conclusions.

The thesis provides the socio-economic background of the informants, and deals with the attitudes and problems of the aged respondents. Finally, the inquiry brings to light the fact that in spite of similarities in age, occupation and resources of the retirees, there is a great heterogeneity in the economic, health and socio-psychological problems and in the patterns of adjustment of the retirees to cope with their aging process and socio-economic conditions. The inquiry also tells how a few retirees are without problems and how they have successful aging.

This study is significant because it tries to clarify and further test some of the theoretical positions that are current in the field of social gerontology, particularly those in India.

I acknowledge the help and guidance I have received from my supervisor, Prof. A. Munirathnam Reddy, Head, Department of Social Anthropology, Sri Venkateswara University, Tirupati in conducting the study and preparing this thesis.

My thanks are due to Dr. P. Balasiddamuni, Lecturer, Department of Statistics, S.V. University, Tirupati for assisting me in conducting the required statistical tests.

My deep sense of acknowledgement is to my friend Mr. K. Rajasekhar for his co-operation in field-work, and for other contingent assistance.

I would also like to thank Prof. G. Prakasam Reddy, Dr. M. Suryanarayana, Dr. P. Sudhakhara Reddy and Mr. V. Gangadhar, Faculty of the Department of Social Anthropology, S.V. University, Tirupati.

My grateful thanks are reserved to my elder sister's husband Dr. V. N. Sastry (late) who has extended a great hand in the process of writing the thesis which includes academic dialogues and discussions towards the attainment of my cherished goal, namely, completion of the thesis.

My deep sense of respect and gratitude goes to my beloved subjects of study for their warm sincerity and active cooperation in collecting the field date.

My special thanks go to the officers in various Departments in Tirupati, the Collectorate in Chittoor and the Secretaries of several caste associations and retirees' associations in Tirupati for their assistance, cooperation and guidance in collecting the number and the general background of the retired employees in Tirupati.

A. ANAND

Hyderabad
January 18, 2004

CONTENTS

PREFACE V

1. INTRODUCTION 1-10
STATEMENT OF THE PROBLEM
OBJECTIVES OF THE STUDY
HYPOTHESES RELATED TO THE STUDY
SIGNIFICANCE OF THE STUDY
LIMITATIONS OF THE SYUDY
ORGANISATION OF THE STUDY
2. REVIEW OF STUDIES ON RETIREMENT 11-28
DIVERSITY OF STUDIES ON RETIREMENT
Areas examined by the studies
Respondents Covered by the studies
STUDIES ON PRE-RETIREMENT CONDITIONS
Institutionalization of retirement
Factors behind retirement
STUDIES ON POST-RETIREMENT CONDITIONS
Psychological changes
Dynamics of adjustment
Patterns of adjustment
Morale dimensions
Attitudes of retirees and society
Health conditions
Family and social relationships
Work and activity

STUDIES ON POST-RETIREMENT PROBLEMS

General problems

Psychological problems

Economic problems

Housing problems

Personality problems

Problems of women retirees

Societal attitudes and retirement problems

Planning for the future of retirees

STUDIES ON RETIREES IN INDIA

Studies on retirees

Respondents chosen by the studies

Studies on pre-retirement conditions

Studies on post-retirement conditions

Studies on post-retirement problems

3. METHODOLOGY 29-41

SAMPLING DESIGN OF THE STUDT
Universe of the study

Sample chosen for the study

DATA GAYHERING PROCESS

Techniques of data collection

Collection of data

ANALYSIS OF DATA

Variables under study

Analysis of aspects of retirement

Statistical tests used for the analysis

4. TIRUPATI: THE TOWN AND ITS PEOPLE 43-56

Social diversity

Physical diversity

RESOURCES OF THE TWON

Changes in the ecological areas

RETIRED EMPLOYEES

Retirees in general

Retirees selected for the study

5. WORK AND RETIREMENT 57-70

WORK
Concept of work

Types of work

The work of work

RETIREMENT

Age of retirement

Event of retirement

Opinion on compulsory retirement

Preparation for retirement

Opinion regarding re-employment

Problems faced at the time of retirement

Work and retirement

6. ECONOMIC ADJUSTMENT 71-91

INCOME

Sources of income

Annual income

Expenditure

Discretion of the aged regarding
Their properties

ANNUAL BUDGETS

Budget heads

Deficit budget

Surplus budget

Balanced budget
Adequency of income

FINANCIAL MANAGEMENT

Financial help received during crises

Social functions and ceremonies
Affecting financial positions
Management of finances

Cause for living with children
After retirement

PATTERNS OF ECONOMIC ADJUSTMENT

Bases and patterns of economic adjustment

The well adjusted

The poorly adjusted

The marginally adjusted

7. FAMILY ADJUSTMENT 93-142

PRESENT FAMILY

Size of the family

Genealogical composition

Type of the family

FAMILY AT THE TIME OF RETIREMENT

Proportions of different types of family

Formation of different types of family

DYNAMICS OF THE FAMILY

Continuity of and change in the family

Continuity of and change in single member domestic units

Continuity of and change in incomplete nuclear families

Continuity of and change in incomplete Nuclear families with dependents

Continuity of and change in complete nuclear Families

Continuity of and change in complete Nuclear families with dependents

Continuity of and change in complete Vertically extended families With dependents

Continuity of and change in horizontally extended families

WORKING OF THE FAMILY

Inter-persona relations

Husband and wives in the family

Parents and children in the family

Grand-parent and grand-child in the family

TYPES OF FAMILIAL ADJUSTMENT

Bases of familial adjustment

Pattern of adjustment to living alone

Pattern of adjustment to a living with Family members with dependency factors associated

8. RELIGIOUS ACTIVITIES AND SOCIO-PSYCHOLOGICAL PROBLEMS 143-170

RELIGIOUS ACTIVITIES OF THE RETIREES

Prayers

Participation in religious activities
utilisation of leisure time

SOCIO-PSYCHOLOGICAL PROBLEMS AND APPROACHES

Social isolation and loneliness

Perception on special position given to them as the aged

Lack of companionship due to death

Ambitions of the retirees

Perception on urbanization

Perception on family type

Family orientations and kin-group relations

Relations with children

Opinion regarding children consulting them on important family matters

Perception on children's approach to traditional values

Best person to decide children's interests

Perception on retirees attitudes to maintain the family

Identification of generation gap

Views on younger generation

Opinion on children's education

Opinion on children's marriages

9. HEALTH CONDITIONS AND PROBLEMS 171-183

HEALTH CONDITIONS BEFORE RETIREMENT

Illness gone through just before

Capacity to bear medical expenses

HEALTH CONDITIONS AFTER RETIREMENT

Health status of the retirees
Difficulties faced in specific activities
Capacity to bear medical expenses
Mental problems of the retirees
Effect of retirement on illness
Addictions of the retires
Reasons attributed to drinking
Smoking and betel leaf chewing
Persons who take care of the retirees
During their illness
10. SUMMARY AND CONCLUSIONS 185-197
APPENDIX-I 199-207
APPENDIX-II 208-210
REFERENCES 211-227

Introduction 1

Social gerontology has taken its roots in psychology and sociology at the beginning of the present century. Since 1910 many psychologists and sociologists have been drawn into research because issues of retired people have come into prominence. The decade between 1920 and 1930 provided an opportunity for making greater endeavour to understand the specific problems of the aged people among the working and non-working populations in the Western Societies. Before the commencement of the Second World War, psychologists and sociologists have made systematic studies not only to understand the social, economic and psychological problems but also to suggest some solutions to the problems of the older people in the Western Societies. Their researches have shown that the problems of the aged people are not a legacy of past nor are they culture specific but rather they are a result of the complex operation of economic, political, social and other factors and that the solutions to the problems are not possible by tinkering with one aspect or the other but need a simultaneous tackling of several aspects of individual, culture and society (Hall 1922: i-ii, Ruch 1933 : 387-414, Miles1933 : i-iii).

After 1953, social gerontology has found a place in many universities and Institutes. Laboratories devoted to the study of aging were started, research societies were formed and many national and international conferences were held. A new kind of scientists began to be seen, one whose major career interest was that of studying the developmental processes and aging. Centers of research, the students of which reflected certain theoretical positions, came to be recognized. A tradition has been thus set for studying the social, economic and psychological aspects of the aged populations in different parts of the world (Miles 1961 : 127-134).

Between 1955 and 1960, anthropologists, demographers and allied social scientists too entered the field of social gerontology and investigated into the culturological, social, demographic, political and religious conditions of the aged people in many parts of the globe (Scott 1955 : 538-546, Clark and Barbara 1967 : i-iii). As a result, social gerontology has acquired its fullness in dealing with the culture, social, psychological, technological, political, economic and religious aspects of its subjects, namely the aged populations in different cultures and settings (Clark and Barbara 1967 : i-iii, Tibbits 1968 : 2-18).

Although social gerontology has formed into a distinct discipline between 1920 and 1960, it could recognize retirement as a significant event with serious possible consequences only between 1950 and 1960, because social scientists who were interested in the study of social gerontology discovered retirement as a potential field of research only in the second half of the present century (Graebner 1978: 2-17, Balles, Reese and Lipsitt 1980 : 31-69). No sooner than the social scientists discovered retirement as a potential field of research, many have ventured to study it with the same gravity and scientific approach as they approached the other subjects. Since the problem of retirement is closely connected with old age, gerontologists and developmental psychologists too have turned their attention to this area (Agruso 1978 : 3-10).

Now, social gerontologists recognise retirement not as an isolated phenomenon but as a phenomenon having biological, geographical, sociological, culturological and psychological links. In universities where social gerontology is taught there is a special division of gerontology with regular courses in pre-retirement education and pre-retirement instruction. The Declaration of United Nations Organisation proclaiming the year of 1982 as the International Year of the Aged had already given an impetus for furthering the study of the retirees. In this context, social gerontology has accepted its dual nature as a discipline and as an applied profession. It is playing an important role in suggesting appropriate services to the retirees and in continuing the research programmes with reference to the retirees.

STATEMENT OF THE PROBLEM

In India, social gerontology is still in its formative stage. Attempts to study the psycho-social conditions of the retirees were made only in 1965. But no serious efforts were made to study the retirees in the past twenty five years. As a result, there are only a handful of studies dealing with the social, economic, religious and psychological conditions of the retirees (Anand 1967, Ramamurthi 1968, 1970, 1982, Joshi 1971, Deo and Bhullar 1974, Walker 1974, Anantaraman 1979, 1981, 1984, Rao and Madhavan 1982, Rangaswami 1983).

However, stirrings of interest in the socio-economic conditions of retirees in urban areas began to become noticeable around 1982. Since then, articles and discussions in press and public have appeared with increasing frequency. Yet, academic bodies like universities and research councils and private bodies such as regional and national associations of pensioners have to take significant steps to undertake research on retirees in India.

In the last one decade there has been a growing awareness of the life and problems of the retirees in India. This awareness has partly been brought about by the information of several regional associations and national organizations of pensioners and partly by the growth of public and private retirement systems in consonance with the technological, economic, social and political changes in Indian society.

In India, the number of older persons aged 60 years and above was 12 millions in 1901, 20 millions in 1951, 24.7 millions in 1961, 32.7 millions in 1971, 43.2 millions in 1981 and it will be 51 millions in 1991 (Yojana 1983: 57-62). According to the Census of India 1981, the percentage of persons 60 years and above is 6.5 and the percentage of workers aged 60 years and above in total working populations is 8.32. Life expectancy in India between 1941 and 1950 was 32.4 years for men and 31.7 years for women. In 1976, it was 50.8 for men and 50 for women. There is an increasing employment of women in different sectors in India (Ranade and Ramachandran 1970, Padmanabha 1983: 4-6). Rising unemployment, greater life-expectancy and an increase in aged population have created a number of social, economic and health problems (Banerjee 1983: 3-14). Technological advances are creating more and more occupations for employees.

Keeping pace with all demographic, social, economic and technological changes, the retirees have become a composite of diversities based upon several objective and subjective factors. Accordingly, their problems also differ from each other (Delhi School of Social Work 1977, Bose 1982, Bhattacharjee 1982, De Souza 1982, Yojana 1983, Banerjee 1983, Hardikar and Bhatia 1983, Times of

India 1983, The Hitawada 1983, Sundaram 1984). In this context, the problems of the gazetted and non-gazetted retirees are often spelt out in striking contrast. The view posited by the gazetted retirees is that retirement has wrought them loss of status, loss of respect, and loss of income and has created a number of economic, social, psychological and physical problems. On the contrary, the view expressed by the non-gazetted retirees is that among the retirees they are the worse sufferers because they have to face more number of social, psychological, economic and physical problems than the gazetted retirees. This polarization of view-points of the two categories of retired employees has become a puzzle to the policy makers, administrators and scientists alike because the standpoints of the gazetted and non-gazetted retirees have not been supported with statistical ammunition and scientific information to document their differential charges against their own conditions and problems (Mamoria 1965, Kapadia 1977, Malik 1980, Nayar 1980).

This puzzle has been regarded as a touchy subject. A review of the literature bears this out. The disinclination to examine this allegedly sensitive issue has had serious consequences for research. It has meant that data of major importance have not been gathered as part of a larger study and the statistics on the gazetted and non-gazetted retirees have been submerged in a mass of the data. Studies made exclusively on retirees over the past twenty years also show that the differential problems and patterns of adjustment of the gazetted and the non-gazetted retirees were rarely the primary focus of investigations. Out the 55 studies made on different occupational categories of retirees over the last two decades, as many as 53 have not covered the gazetted and non-gazetted differences in their investigations relating to the trends in adjustment (Ramamurthi 1965, 1968, 1970, 1976, 1982, Paintal 1979, Anantaraman 1981), bodily dysfunctions and general health problems (Joshi 1972), family and social relationships (Soodan 1972), work and activity level (Sharma 1971), problems related to pension, family life, proximity of friends, anxiety and insecurity (Deoras and Janabandhu 1984), and attitudes and problems (Menachery 1987), and only 2 studies have elucidated the patterns of semblance and difference in the social, economic, religious, recreational and health problems of the gazetted and non-gazetted retirees (Desai 1970, Bhatia 1983). This finding and analyses in these two studies are in correspondence with the view that there are significant differences in the problems and adjustment of the gazetted and non-gazetted retirees(Desai 1970, Madras School of Social Work, 1972, University of Lucknow 1978, Maharashtra Herald 1983, 1984). they also synchronize with the deliberations of some of the gerontological conferences, workshops and discussions (Munjal 1974, Dayal, Madgaonkar and Dhasandraiah 1983, Menachery 1983, 1984, 1985).

Clearly, the available studies do not provide comparable data for all the gazetted and non-gazetted retirees in different localities, regions and zones of India. Statistical coverage of incomes of both the categories of the retirees is spotty and the picture remains incomplete. From what can be pieced together, the gazetted retirees with higher incomes seem to adjust economically better than the non-gazetted retirees with lower incomes. Generally, the socio-economic adjustment of the non-gazetted retirees makes a poor showing in contrast to that of the gazetted retirees. The two systematic studies which compared the conditions and problems of the gazetted and non-gazetted are illustrative, but neither of these give a holistic picture of the problems of the gazetted and non-gazetted retirees (Desai1970, Bhatia 1983). To be brief, the data available on the socio-economic differentials and problems of the gazetted and non-gazetted retirees remain fragmentary. Caution has to be applied in generalizing from the data. The paucity of research on the gazetted and non-gazetted retirees in India, therefore, permits to a need for further data collection and analysis in order to ascertain some of the variables related to the socio-economic conditions, attitudes and problems of the gazetted and non-gazetted retirees in urban areas that embrace a vast majority of the retired employees.

Planners, policy-makers, administrators and social gerontologists have also now identified through investigation into the economic, social, physical and psychological conditions of the gazetted and non-gazetted retirees as a top priority area of research. At a time when work has become a central life task as well as a source of income, when demographic shifts have brought rising unemployment, greater life expectancy and an increase in olderly populance and when the economic and political climate, both locally and nationally, has brought fiscal restrictions to meet the needs of the aged populations, it is fitting to examine and to grasp fully the differential economic, social, physical and psychological problems of the gazetted and non-gazetted retirees in different parts of the country for the purpose of developing certain strategies for post-retirement life of the gazetted and non-gazetted retirees in different parts of the country for the purpose of developing certain strategies for post-retirement life of the gazetted and non-gazetted categories of employees. It is in the light of these reasons the present enquiry is formulated.

The present inquiry is an in-depth study of the gazetted and non-gazetted retirees in Tirupati, a pilgrim-town located in the north-eastern part of Chittoor District in the State of Andhra Pradesh. It focuses its attention on the following lines. What exactly is the working man complex among the gazetted and non-gazetted employees? What is its influence on retirement? How does retirement represent an economically non-productive role for the retirees whose labour is not considered essential or necessary for the functioning of the economic order? Although economically , while departure from life-long career serves as the basic operational indicator of retirement, sociologically how retirement becomes a prescribed transition from a position of an economically active person in accordance with the norms through which society defines and determines the nature of this change? How do the gazetted and non-gazetted retirees face an instantaneous fall in income and social contacts? What are the similarities and differences in the patterns of adjustment of the gazetted and non-gazetted retirees? Is the post-retirement adjustment of the gazetted or non-gazetted retirees homogeneous or heterogeneous? If heterogeneous, what factors are responsible for creating the diversity in the patterns of adjustment within the gazetted category or non-gazetted category of retirees? Accordingly, what needs to be considered is not only the question of gazetted and non-gazetted status differentials, but how the diversity in socio-economic standing of the gazetted or non-gazetted retirees generates heterogeneous patterns of adjustment within the gazetted category or within the non-gazetted category of retirees.

In addition to examining all these aspects of the post-retirement life of the gazetted and non-gazetted employees, the present study highlights the social, economic and health problems of the gazetted and non-gazetted retirees in an urban setting.

OBJECTIVES OF THE STUDY

The overall objective of the study is to know the patterns of semblance and difference with reference to the socio-economic conditions, problems and adjustment of the gazetted and non-gazetted retirees in Tirupati. The specific objectives of the present enquiry are:

i. To understand the working man complex among the gazetted and non-gazetted employees;

ii. To know the different factors that are responsible for making retirement of the gazetted and non–gazetted employees as a social phenomenon;

iii. To know the differential attitudes of the gazetted and non-gazetted retirees from different occupational categories towards mandatory age for retirement and preparation for retirement;

iv. To examine the socio-economic conditions of the gazetted and non-gazetted retirees in terms of family, kin, authority, financial control, decision making and inter-personal relations, in terms of occupation, income, expenditure, savings and property, and in terms of health conditions, entertainment, leisure time activities and religious interests; and

v. To identify the economic, health and socio-psychological problems affecting the life and adjustment of the gazeted and non-gazetted retirees.

The present inquiry is a case study of the retirees. It enables the investigator to collect the relevant empirical data in support of the above mentioned objectives regarding the social, psychological, economic, political, religious and other implications of retirement of different categories of employees in an Indian town.

HYPOTHESES RELATED TO THE STUDY

The study focuses its attention on variables which seem to correlate with occupation, income, physical condition and satisfaction with life in order to at least partially account for the similarities and differences in the socio-economic conditions, problems and adjustments of the gazetted and non-gazetted retirees. In this connection, the following hypotheses are formulated and tested:

H1 Employees who want immediate retirement tend to show less satisfaction with life in general than do the employees who continue to work even after retirement.

H2 Income level influences the choices of the retirees either for re-employment or withdrawal from work.

H3 Retirees in the more highly paid occupations have more savings and other resources for retirement income than do retirees in the jobs drawing lower pay.

H4 Retirees, who are energetic and continue to work, play a greater role in maintaining their families than others.

H5 Retirees with higher income and more domestic responsibilities play a dominant role in maintaining their families.

H6 Gazetted retirees by virtue of their better educational levels have greater sophistication to socio-psychological issues than the non-gazetted retirees.

H7 There is a considerable gap in the attitudinal approach of the gazetted and non-gazetted retirees to different issues which include children's education and marriage.

H8 Financial constraints after retirement make the retired employee seek re-employment.

SIGNIFICANCE OF THE STUDY

The studies on the gazetted and non-gazetted retirees have been largely descriptive , documenting the socio-economic differences but not providing reasons for the differences in the socio-economic conditions, attitudes and problems of the gazetted and non-gazetted retirees. The present study is significant because it moves a step beyond description to explanation.

This study is also significant because it tries to clarify and further test some of the theoretical positions that are current in the field of social gerontology, particularly those in India.

Further, the present study is significant for it points out to the need for an integrated approach to an understanding of the social, cultural, economic and other aspects of the life of the gazetted and non-gazetted retirees.

LIMITATIONS OF THE STUDY

The present study is limited in the following ways:

i. It examines in depth the retirees in the urban area of Tirupati.

So, it does not include the rural places around Tirupati.

ii. It considers only those employees who are retired from government, quasi-government, and private organizations. It does not cover retirees from a single organization.

iii. It deals with retirees whose background in terms of caste, class, occupation and religion is different. The findings do not pertain to retirees belonging to a single caste, single occupation or single religious faith.

iv. It has drawn a sample which includes 200 respondents of whom 10 are females and 190 are males. It is more a study of male retirees.

ORGANISATION OF THE STUDY

The present study is organized into ten chapters.

CHAPTER-1 is introductory. It deals with the orientation and limitations of the study.

CHAPTR-2 surveys the available literature on retirees with special reference to pre-retirement conditions, post-retirement changes and problems of retirees besides approaches to the study of retirees.

CHAPTER-3 describes the methodology adopted for studying the sample respondents. It gives the research design in accordance with the objectives of study and the hypotheses formulated for the study.

CHAPTERS-4 and 5 depict the background of the retirees, deal with the working man complex of the gazetted and non-gazetted employees, and describes retirement as a social and economic event. The depiction takes into consideration the first three objectives of the study.

CHAPTER-6 deals with the economic adjustment in retired life. It examines the sources, levels and adequacy of income of the retirees, adjustment of income to economic needs in terms of reduction in wants and needs, utilization of saving, financial problems on account of social customs, and finally patterns of economic adjustment by the retirees.

CHAPTER-7 focusses its attention on the familial adjustment, composition, inter-personal relations and working of the families of the retirees. The analysis highlights the dynamics of the family.

CHAPTER-8 is about the religious activities and socio-psychological problems of the retirees. It gives an account of the leisure time activities, types of entertainment, religious activities and psychological side of the retirement life.

The analysis of data in CHAPTERS 5-9 fulfils the fourth and fifth objectives of the present enquiry.

CHAPTER-9 is about the health conditions and the health care taken by the retirees with an emphasis on the physical problems currently faced by the retirees.

CHAPTER-10 summarises the findings and gives some conclusions. It examines the implications of the findings at the conceptual, methodological and theoretical level and at the level of planning for the welfare of the gazetted and non-gazetted retirees.

Review of Studies on Retirement

2

This chapter presents a review of literature related to retirees in different parts of the world and in India.

First, it reviews the studies made so far in several countries other than India. The review reveals that the studies in different countries are related to pre-retirement conditions, post-retirement conditions, problems of retirement and planning for the adjustment of retirees.

Secondly, it reviews the studies made on retirees in India. The review shows the paucity of research on retirees in India, the concentration of the research only on two areas, viz., post-retirement conditions and problems of retirement, and the absence of specific studies on pre-retirement conditions and planning for the adjustment of retirees.

DIVERSITY OF STUDIES ON RETIREES

Areas examined by the studies

Studies so far made on the retired employees or workers reveal four broad areas of research: pre-retirement conditions, post-retirement conditions, problems of retirement and planning for the adjustment of retirees.

Studies on pre-retirement conditions focused their attention on institutionalization of retirement and factors behind the institutionalized retirement.

Researches on post-retirement conditions examined psychological changes, dynamics of adjustment, patterns of adjustment, morale dimensions, attitudes, health conditions and family and social relationships.

Investigations into post-retirement problems reveal general, psychological, economic, housing and personality problems besides problems of women retirees, problems of immigrant retirees and societal attitudes as creators of the problems of retirees.

Literature available on planning for the adjustment of retirees covers two topics namely the arguments for and against mandatory age of retirement and the programmes and plans to develop strategies for post-retirement life.

Respondents covered by the studies

The respondents chosen by the studies are those aged 50 years and above, 55 years and above, 60 years and above and 70 years and above.

Among the subjects selected by the studies, about 90 percent are retirees between 55 years and above 70 years, nearly 5 percent are between 50 and 55 years who are on the verge of retirement, and the remaining 5 percent are women of whom about 3 percent are retirees aged between 55 years and above 70 years and 2 percent are aged between 50 and 55 years and on the brink of retirement.

All studies except four covered samples of retirees or workers in urban centers. Three studies, one from Japan (Kikuchi, Sai and Ooe 1975) and two from India, (Purohit and Sharma 1972, Marula Siddaiah 1972) covered aged people in a fishing village and a few agricultural villages respectively. Another study from Germany, (Szwarch 1981) included urban and rural respondents in its sample.

The respondents of the studies included several occupational, income level, religious and other categories of people in towns and cities: doctors, lawyers, journalists, executives, teachers, telephone company employees, steel, workers, coal miners, skilled craftsman, retail sales persons, church members, church leaders, hospitalized people, disabled people, institutionalized and non-institutionalized persons besides non-working aged men and women in towns and cities.

Most of the respondents are whites in the urban centers of western countries. Some are blacks in the cities of U.S.A. An overwhelming number of the subjects are Christians and the remaining subjects included people from Bangladesh, (Chaudury 1982), India (Menachery 1987), Israel (Eran 1976), Nepal (Sharma), Japan, Russia (Shapiro & Pyshor 1979) and the Chinese and Japanese settled in the United States of America, (Kalish and Moriwak 1973).

The size of the sample respondents chosen for different studies varied according to the objectives stated, variables to be examined and tools of research adopted by the inquiries. It was less than 100 individuals in more than 150 researches, between 100 and 500 in 20 researches, and from 501 and 1000 individuals in 25 researches and between 1001 and 6000 persons in about 5 researches.

STUDIES ON PRE-RETIREMENT CONDITIONS

Institutionalization of retirement

Researches related to the institutionalization of retirement reveal how all those societies with a brief history came to have retirement as a social institution and how retirement has become a social problem where societies have become more and more industrialized – (Gubrium 1976: 178, Telford and Sawrrey 1977: 499, Graebner 1980: 3-7, Tibbits 1983: 7-14). Further, some of these researches reveal that retirement is a traumatic experience (Buhler 1973: 895), a time of crisis (Zinberg, Norman and Kaufman 1963: 46, Geist 1968: 26) and a complete withdrawal from employment (Atchley 1982: 26). However, some of the researches show that retirement is not a crisis because it does not always imply a loss of status, respect, health and job opportunity and that retirement provides greater freedom and flexibility, a respite from tight schedule, and a time to reorganize one's life and interests (Goode 1977:453). A great majority of the researches have concluded that retirement is a process of adjustment and that the crisis of retirement can be ameliorated by substitute satisfactions (Simpson and McKinney1966).

Orbach, while examining the factors that have led to the institutionalization of retirement, concludes that the development of retirement is related to technological, social, political and demographic changes in modern society. He summarizes these developments into four categories viz. (i) creation of technology based on scientific approach, (ii) order through powerful national states, (iii) a unique demographic revolution, and (iv) the reorganization of man's economic and social life (Orbach 1968: 390).

Further, Orbach writes "Retirement represents the creation in modern society of an reconomically non-productive role for large numbers of persons whose labour is not considered essential or necessary for the functioning of the economic order. While departure from life-long career may serve as the basic operational indicator of retirement, sociologically retirement raises problems of dynamics of social and institutional roles and relationships of a more basic structure than those associated with mere occupational change. As a social process, retirement is the prescribed transition from a position of an economically active person to that of an economically non-active person in accordance with the norms through which the society defines and determines the nature of this change (Ibid 1973 : 53).

Factors behind retirement

Studies related to the factors behind retirement as a social phenomenon show the development of retirement as a result of societal changes (Bromley,1966: 73, Orbach 1968: 370) changes in demographic structure in terms of rise in life-expectancy and the consequent socio-economic implications, (Slavick, Smith, Shultz and Mc Connell 1968 : 261, Buhler 1973: 895, Green, Parham , Kleff and Pillisuk, 1980: 1-7) increasing participation of women in the labour force, (Havighurst 1973: 602, Semyonov 1980: 534-550), technological advances in terms of high skills, demand for energetic skilled personnel and early and compulsory retirement practices, (Gubrium 1976:198, Telford and Sawrey 1977: 499).

From agrarian sector to industrial sector and subsequent formation of industrial and bureaucratic working class besides organization of rules and regulations for mandatory rejection of employees who reach a specific age and creation of new roles and life-styles for the rejected employees (Orbach 1968 : 53, Williams 1963 : 290, Gubrium 1976 : 198), workingman complex which denotes a beginning and ending of one's economic and social life based on specific work or career patterns and specific time schedules, (Maddox 1968:357, Chown 1977: 682, Kreps 1979: 13-18), productive role of working men as against the non-productive life of aged people, (Strauss, Aldrichand Lipman 19767:221, Wood 1980: 783-807), changes in the family structure favouring neolocal residence patterns, erosion of authority of the aged in family decision-making, intolerance of younger generations to accommodate dependents and age segragation in the urban family (Gillin, DittmerColbert and Kastier 1965: 11-42) and new cultural values and youth-oriented culture in which the older people find themselves unfit and begin to withdraw into their own world. (Zinberg and Kaufman 1963: 40-47, Hunter 1975: 276-277).

STUDIES ON POST-RETIREMENT CONDITIONS

Psychological changes

Investigations into the psychological changes of the retirees reveal self-perception in terms of more hostility and aggressive behaviour, (Prestone 1966: 415-420), denial of ill-health, (Shstcut 1958), symptoms of depressions (Brink 1977:10-11, Broomley 1977 : 104-111, Anand 1967: 391-396), psychoneurotic signs and symptoms (Asnes and Shulman 1976: 237- 253) and context specific alienation (Martin, Bengtson, Vern and Alean 1974: 265- 274, Menachery 1987: 26) among the retirees.

Dynamics of adjustment

Empirical studies on the dynamics of adjustment in retirement show that healthy adjustment or maladjustment is a cumulative result of many factors like age, health, self-concept, activity level, religious beliefs, attitudes, and type of occupations.

The relevant findings, reveal decline in adjustment as age increases (Paintal 1979: 27-33), a deterioration in adjustment around the period of retirement followed by an improvement till the mid-sixties and thereafter a gradual decline in adjustment which becomes marked after the age of seventy among the urban retirees (Ramamurthi 1976: 41-44), better adjustment of those with positive self-concept than those with negative self–concept among the urban retirees (Anantaraman 1981: 46-50), significantly better adjustment of normal individuals in contrast with those who are hospitalized patients or those who have physical problems among the urban retirees (Mukherjee 1980:11-13, Anantaraman 1981: 46-50), healthy adjustment of elderly women who have happy marital life in contrast with the maladjusted elderly women who have no marital happiness (Busse and Eisdorfer 1970: 266-269), healthier adjustment of urban retirees with many religious activities than those with a few religious activities (Moberg 1953: 87-90), significant differences in the adjustment of institutionalized and non-institutionalized aged persons among the urban retirees (Paintal 1976: 101-109), better adjustment of the urban retirees who have greater number of close friends and effective interaction with them (Paintal 1976: 101-109), linkage between activity level and high morale, (Cumming, Dean, Newell and McCaffrey 1960: 23-25), better adjustment of those with voluntary disengagement than those with forced disengagement (Lowenthal and Boler 1965: 284 - 301), successful adjustment dependent upon greater need fulfilment activity than mere activeness (Reichard, Livson and Paterson 1968: 198), heterogeneity of adjustment varying in accordance with the type of occupation (Friedman & Havighurst 1954), less retirement anxieties among doctors, lawyers and journalists who can continue their profession even after retirement (Paintal 1979: 27-33) and better adjustment of women retirees than men retirees (Atchley 1982: 266-287).

Patterns of adjustment

The empirical findings have also brought out the patterns of adjustment of the retirees. The contrasting patterns of adjustment categorise the retirees into well-adjusted and maladjusted. Indepth analysis of these two categories of people in terms of individual differences in role profiles and levels of social interaction reveals several patterns and sub-patterns of adjustment: retirees with `people oriented' adjustment who are concerned with human relationships as against retirees with `task- oriented' adjustment who are concerned with more role play, greater life satisfaction, less anomie and isolation and more leisure activities (William and Wirths 1965), retirees with `task oriented' adjustment in terms of their positive satisfaction, energetic nature and living to deal with uncertainity and a change against retirees with `nontask-oriented' adjustment in terms of their avoidance of dissatisfaction, preference to the placid and quiet and dislike to deal with uncertainity and change (Hamlin 1967: 37-45), retirees who are `transformers' and retirees who are `maintainers' in accordance with their patterns of responses to social interactions (Snow and Havighurst 1977: 545-552) `matured people' rocking chair' men, `armoured' people, `angry men', and the `self –haters' in terms of their personal characteristics related to good adjustment and poor adjustment (Bromley 1966: 104-111, Reichard, Livson and Paterson 1968: 178-179, Buhler, Keith-Spiegel and Thomas 1973: 895).

Morale dimensions

Researches into the morale or life satisfaction aspect of the retirees depict that morale is lower among the retirees than among those still working (Chown 1977: 683) and morale is higher among the voluntarily withdrawn retirees but low among the involuntarily withdrawn retirees (Lowenthal and Boler 1972: 284-301).

Attitudes of retirees and society

Several researches are made on attitudes of the retirees on various issues and on attitudes of society towards retirees. These studies observe that old age is looked as a period characterized by economic insecurity, poor health, loneliness, resistance to change and indifferent feelings towards physical and mental powers (Tuckman and Lorge 1952 : 137-149), that a vast majority of the retirees have fear of death (Jeffers, Nichols & Eisdorfer 1970: 395-401), that dependent people in society have a favourable attitude towards deprived people among the retirees (Kogan & Wallagh 1961: 272-280), that the strongest attitudinal cluster of the retirees is anomie (Lowenthal and Boler 1972: 284-301) that negative labelling and stigmatization of the elderly contribute to behaviour that actually confirm the prevalent stereotypes of old age and lead to lower self-esteem and diminished feelings of control (Rodin and Langer 1980: 12-29), that work satisfaction necessitates pre-retirement planning for those having different work-retirement attitudes (Goudy, Powers and Keith 1975: 267-279), that people with satisfaction in retirement are more likely to have favourable attitudes towards retirement than others (Streib and Thompson 1957: 180-191), that husbands look forward to retirement more than their wives do (Kerchhoff 1972: 312-328), that feelings about oneself as young, healthy and effective are stronger determinants of favourable attitudes toward retirement than perceptions of the job (Eden and Jacobson 1976: 145-154) and that retirees in good health, with social involvement, enough money and a sense of worth have no greater problems than they did at their younger age (Keily, Dudek and Stephaine 1977: 181-184).

Health conditions

Health of the retirees is another area which attracted the attention of social gerontologists. The researches in this regard reveal a significant correlation between a person's health and his material situation among both urban and rural retirees (Szwarch 1981: 280), association of specific bodily dysfunctions with aging and retirement (Joshi 1971: 64-68, Hayslip and panek 1983: 479-485), death of lower status workers within three years after their retirement and death of higher status orders four to five years after retirement (Haynes, McMichael and Tyroler 1977: 105-114) health, mental abilities and satisfying social roles as the most important promoters of longevity of the retirees (Palmore 1969: 103-108) and biological aging process decreases the activity and physical strength and poor economic conditions aggravate the poor health of the aged persons (Mahajan 1987: 36).

Family and Social relationships

Family and social relationships is another domain covered by the researches in social gerontology. The studies reveal loss, maintenance or gain of social status after retirement (Strauss, Aldricch and Lipman 1976), a vast majority of the families with women who lost their aged husbands, absence of role play for many aged retirees in maintaining their families, and restriction of role play of retirees to assistance but not to responsibility (Soodan 1972: 50-52), primary group interaction based on the relative with whom most visits of the retirees take place and possible contribution of primary group interaction to feelings of uselessness on the part of the retirees (Hampe and Blevins 1975: 309-320), predominance of separate dwelling pattern for aged retirees and at the same time maintenance of close ties between aged retirees and their offspring highlighting mutual affection and some measure of dependence (Brown 1970), and some indication that retirees with high level of education and relatively high socio-economic status are likely to possess greater internal and external resources so that regardless of age and retirement, highly uniform social participation patterns and interests may prevail (Geist 1968: 53).

Work and Activity

Work and activity of the retirees is one area which is covered by a large number of researches. However, the researches show many conflicting results. They reveal early retirement of unskilled workers and late retirement of professionals and semi-professionals (Uhlig 1952: 90-93), lower retirement rate of men in the better paid occupations and higher retirement rate of men in the low paid occupations (Menachery 1987: 38), differential repercussions in retirement due to differential meaning of work for different categories of workers (Friedman and Havighurst 1963, Havighurst 1963), choice between continued employment or immediate retirement as a function of the difference between the individual outcomes concerned, (Eran 1976: 605-610), preference of the retirees to perform specific activities (Sharma 1971: 76-77), higher total activity scores for men retirees than for women retirees (Rowe 1976 : 456-461, Palmore 1980:321-341, Heyman and Jeffers 1970: 310-

318), irregular work experiences of older male and female retirees (Quadagno 1978: 55-74), higher morale among the older working females than among the retired females and higher morale among the desired females than among the females who never worked (Jaslow 1976: 212-218), advantage of working female retirees over non-working older females in terms of number of social resources at their disposal(Fox 1977: 192-202), and association of high positive work-orientation with negative adjustment among women retirees (Achley 1982: 199-208).

STUDIES ON POST-RETIREMENT PROBLEMS

General Problems

Studies on post-retirement problems deal with general and specific problems of the retirees. So far as the general problems of the retirees are concerned, the researches show that the problems cluster around pension, family life, proximity of friends, anxiety and security (Deoras and Janabandhu 1979), the greater problems pertain to finance, health and personality (Ramamurthi 1970: 128-130), unemployment, withdrawal from active community and organizational leadership, breaking up of marriage through death of one's mate, loss of an independent household, loss of interest in different goals and plans, acceptance of dependence upon others for support or advice, and management of funds, acceptance of a subordinate position to adult offspring or to social workers, taking up of membership in groups made up of largely old people, and acceptance of planning in terms of immediate goals (Menachery 1987:14-15).

Researches related to the general problems of the retirees also reveal biological changes such as lowering of energy levels, changes in physical appearance, changes in intellectual functioning, an overall decline in health and uncertainty about the duration of life (Clark and Barbara 1967, Chappel and Havens 1980:157-171).

Investigations into the general problems explain separation on account of divorce or death of a life partner as a common precursor to a wide spectrum of mental and physiological pathologies (Pillisuk and Minkler 1980:95-116). They also demonstrate negative effects of bereavement in terms of stress created, by moving away from social, cultural and occupational environments and increase in the vulnerability of an individual created by loss of social support (Parkes, Benjamin and Fitzerald 1969:740). They explain social support as a protector against `role shock' among the retirees (Lowenthal and Haven 1960: 385-394), consequences of change of locality as a result of retirement especially when the individual is not prepared for it (Aldrich and Mendhoff 1983: 401-408), and measurement of one's preoccupation over the imminent loss of work not in terms of economic loss but more so in terms of moral and spiritual loss since the meaning attached to one's occupation has numerous non-economic significances (Hunter 1975: 275-277).

Psychological problems

Empirical studies on the psychological problems of the retirees show retirement as a source of anxiety (Rao and Malathi 1972 : 319-332), deterioration in the performance level among persons near retirement (Zinberg and Kaufman 1963: 46), reduction in feelings of confidence and personal worth among the retirees as they are cut off from participation in the most important interests and activities of the society (Strauss, Aldrich and Lipman 1976:220-223), problems of dependency on others as the retirees are called on to play a subordinate function both in the family and in the society (Geist 1968: 22, 53), compulsion on retirees to cope with the changing values, new styles of living , and aggressive challenges of the outside world to establish their authority in the society (Kalish & Moriwak 1973: 187-209), social force on the retirees to identify themselves away from the mainstream (LeCourse and Roy 1982: 25-35), distress at the impending death and environmental stress (Weisman and Kastenbaum 1968) and attitude towards death as a general agitation in the environmental stress (Kastenbaum and Costa 1977:225-249).

Economic problems

Studies on the economic aspect of the retirees have identified several economic problems. They observe that the most frequently cited problem of the retirees is income and the largest portion of the retirees' income is spent on food, followed by rent on mortgage, other housing expenses and transportation (Berger, Young and Heebner 1982: 31-32).

Researches on the economic problems of the retirees have further shown that financial constraints in both the developed and developing nations are making the life of the retirees difficult (Straus, Aldrich and Lipman 1976: 220-221,Malik 1980: 298-303), that the changed policies of social security benefits are making many individuals fear of getting inadequate money at the time of retirement (Time 1981: 19th October), and that the present cost of living and rate of inflation force the retirees receive income that is grossly inadequate to meet their economic needs (Ibid).

Housing problems

Studies related to various problems of the retirees emphasize the physical need for housing the retirees. All researches highlight the close relationship between housing arrangements and the mental health and adjustment (Telford and Sawrey 1976 : 506-509).

The relevant investigations identify the sociological problems arising out of retirement communities (Geist 1968 : 134), the psychological impact of the physical lay-out of apartments (Kleemeier 1961 : 445-446), the theoretical basis of retirement communities (Rosow 1962: 330), the models of new settings (Moos 1982: 40-50), emotional and personal loss on account of bureaucratic structure of nursing homes (Wack and Robin 1978 : 6-21, Blum and Minkler 1980: 133-152), approach towards retirement homes (Brink 1977: 10-11), and finally the relationship between attitudes towards housing arrangement and adjustment of the individual retirees (Telford and Sawrey 1976: 506-509).

A few investigations have also studied housing in relation to retirement and migration. In many countries certain cities have become the predominant destinations for migration of the retirees. Such cities are the centers of retirement life. Retirees migrate to such places for permanent settlement. Researches have shown that migration in the last stage of work is related to retirement and concern for more congenial social community, for climatic situation and for health (Chavan and Fischer 12979: 1369-1380).

Personality problems

A few researches on retirees have highlighted how some problems of retirement and old age are rooted in the personality of retirees. They categorise the personalities of the retirees into three: the `obsessive person' for whom work is everything; the `indulgent person' who makes an excessive libidinal investment in the subject of his work that separation results in the same kind of depression that results from the loss of a loved one; and the third type of person used his work as a way of feeling useful and important. For the first type of person a time without work is unthinkable; for the second type of person doing his work is the sole satisfaction he gets and nothing can substitute it; and for the third type of person retirement creates worthlessness and emptiness in him (Zinberg and Kaufman 1963: 46-47).

The investigations show that retirement is not a problem to those whose work lies in creative fields and to those who have a purely instrumental approach to work. Those who have a wider range of interests and find their psychological satisfaction in other realms are not disturbed at the advent of retirement. Blue and White Collar workers, whose job is associated with particular skills, tools and social techniques take longer time to learn to live without all these (Menachery 1987 : 20-21).

Problems of women retiree

According to available researches women retirees suffer from negative effects of their stigmatized social and economic status (Chappel and Havens 1980 : 157-171).

The researches have shown that as more and more women enter the social and occupational world, problems connected with retirement and occupation are bound to arise. In this connection, it is observed that when the young women of today reach retirement age they will be better off financially and more independent socially and psychologically (Pross 1979 : 132-142).

Problems of retired migrants

Studies on those who migrated to other countries and retired there have shown that they suffer from specific problems: the conflict between two sets of social values; the confrontation with changing styles, changing values, changing house, changing spouse and changing jobs; the loss of hope to return to motherland after growing rich and to spend leisure time with superior status; and the loss of status with reference to the family and community (Kalish and Moriwak 1973: 187-209).

Some studies have shown how certain places within a country have become predominant destinations for retirees and how certain problems of adjustment arise between the retirees and the inhabitants of those places (Chavan & Fischer 1979: 1369-1380).

Societal attitudes and retirement problems

Several studies have shown that societal attitudes in terms of prejudices against the retired, against old age, and against aging process, in terms of discriminating practices against the aged employees, and in terms of institutional practices and policies which perpetuate stereotypic beliefs about the aged, reduce the opportunities of retirees for a satisfactory life and undermine their personal dignity (Butler 1980: 8-11).

Empirical studies have explained how stereotypic behaviour accentuates the tendency to exaggerate most of the physical symptoms to aging and how such physical symptoms are considered as inevitable and hence no remedial steps are taken by the society (Rodin and Langer 1980: 12-19).

STUDIES ON THE FUTURE OF RETIREES

Age of retirement

Researches on age of retirement are not many. The available literature highlights arguments for and against fixing an age for retirement (Barker 1951: 78, Maddox 1968: 358), attitudes of persons and different occupational levels towards retirement age (Hyden 1963: 403-409, Heron and Chown 1970), and attitudinal changes over the years with regard to Mandatory age of retirement (Ekerdt 1976: 161-169).

Recent events in Andhra Pradesh reveal the extent to which age of retirement can play a role even in politics. When one Chief Minister lowered the retirement age of the state employees from 58 years to 55, the next Chief Minister immediately raised the retirement age from 55 to 58 years. Latter when the former Chief Minister was reinstated he preferred to keep the status quo.

Planning for the future of the retirees

There is paucity of research in the field of planning for the future of retirees. The studies available in this regard emphasize the need for preplanning and adjustment (Fuller & Redfering 1976: 497-487), the counseling problems in retirement assistance (Schlenoff 1977 : 103-109), attitudinal changes as a result of pre-retirement planning programmes (Wright, Bennett, Simon and Weinberg 1977: 67-82), adult education programme participation and ease of participation (Bynum, Cooper & Acuff 1978: 253-261), and information sources and interpersonal influence during transition to retirement (Borsay and Anderson 1976).

Some studies have focused their attention on the change that should be brought in the societal attitudes. In this context Wack and Rodin say that changing the societal attitudes is the first step in?—the process of rehabilitation. This is crucial because ultimately it is these social attitudes and stereotypes that pervade the policy making process and shape legislations that will determine retirement programmes (Wack and Rodin 1978).

Several researches have shown that retirement is an outcome of the interplay of diverse factors like social standing, retirement role, cultural values, social expectations and personality make-up and that these factors go to make either a well adjusted person or a highly anomic and disorganized one in retirement (Menachery 1987 : 14).

Some of the researches have emphasized that changing the stereotypes and attitudes of the retirees and society is the crucial step in the process of rehabilitation because ultimately it is these social attitudes and stereotypes that pervade the policy-making and shape legislation that will determine retirement programme (Wack & Rodin 1978 : 6-21).

Many investigations have proposed programmes to prepare the retirees and plan their future in advance. These programmes include pre-retirement counseling (Sinick 1976 : 18-25, Entine 1977 : 332-333), re-employment (Waters and Goodman 1977 : 337-343), development of new pedagogy for pre-retirement education (Mayer 1977 : 115-122), and information bureaus (Radebold 1977 : 73-80). All these researches provide certain strategies for post-retirement life.

STUDIES ON RETIREES IN INDIA

Though social gerontology is still in its infancy in India, ``a great interest is seen in the study of retirement and old age, and this can be seen from the increase in the number of associations of retired persons and centers of study on aging" (Menachery 1987: 3).

As studies in social gerontology started studying the social, economic, familial, and psychological aspects of retirement, they started attracting various disciplines like sociology, anthropology, social work, demography and other disciplines to cover several aspects of retirement in India.

In India, there is no research related to the study of pre-retirement conditions (Appendix – I).

However, many of the researches have focussed their attention on the post-retirement conditions and problems. In this regard, the studies specifically dealt with psychological changes, dynamics of adjustment, health, family and social relationships. The research deals with general problems like psycho-social changes. The specific area of psychological problems deal with the question of retirement as a source of anxiety and dependency. Research on the future of retirees is yet to be undertaken in India.

Studies on retirees

As things stand today scientific studies of aging in India are few (Jamuna & Ramamurthy 1984 : 145-218).

A survey of researches on retirees in India reveals that there are not more than 70 studies on aged people and of these only 2 are related to villages in Karnataka (Marula Siddaiah 1972) and Rajasthan (Pruohit and Sharma 1972) and the remaining 68 are related to retirees in urban centers in Tamil Nadu (Ramamurthi 1965, 1968, Anantaraman 1971, 1984, Rao & Malathi 1980, Rao & Madhavan 1982), Andhra Pradesh (Ramamurthi 1970, 1976, 1982, Jamuna & Ramamurthi 1984), Karnataka (Anantaraman 1981), Maharashtra (Desai & Naik 1970, Menachery 1987), Rajasthan (Sati 1982, Sharma 1978, Bhatia 1983), Madhya Pradesh (Bharat Pensioners Samaj 1971), Uttar Pradesh (Soodan 1972, Singh 1975) and a few other states.

Some researches focused their attention on the demographic trends in the aged population in India (Bose 1982 : 1-19) other researches covered psychological, social, economic and health aspects of the retirees.

Respondents chosen by the studies

Among the respondents few were rural aged people and a vast majority were urban people. Among the aged urban respondents many were retirees and a small number were those who were at the verge or retirement.

The respondents were men aged between 45 and 75 years. Those aged between 45 and 54 years were in the pre-retirement stage and those aged between 55 and 75 years were retirees.

Among the chosen respondents a vast majority were Hindus

and the rest included Christians, Muslims and others.

There was heterogeneity of the subjects. There were gazetted and non-gazetted retirees, medical men, teachers, different categories of workers and hospitalized patients.

The number of subjects selected for the inquiry varied from 44 to 400 individuals. Most of the studies examined less than 100 respondents and about a dozen studies selected 100 to 400 subjects.

Studies on pre-retirement conditions

A survey of the research literature on retirees reveals absence of specific studies on the pre-retirement conditions of the aged people. Although there are a few studies, they are not clearly pin-pointing the pre-retirement conditions for they are hidden in the mass of data on various aspects surrounding retirement.

Studies on post-retirement conditions

Studies on post-retirement conditions are available in a small number. There is only one study which deals with the psychological changes. It observes that retired men suffer from the symptoms of anxiety (Anand 1967 : 391-396).

Some studies examined the adjustment of aged people after their retirement. They have shown a deterioration in adjustment around the period of retirement followed by an improvement till the mid-sixties and thereafter a gradual decline in adjustment which becomes marked after the age of seventy (Ramamurthi 1970 : 128 – 130), correlation between self-concept and adjustment (Anantaraman 1981: 46-50), a negative relationship between the adjustment and anxiety of the normal as well as hospitalized individual (Mukherjee & Upadhyay 1980: 11-13), better health adjustment of those with good or excellent health, with no change in health and with no physical problems (Anantaraman 1981 : 46-50) and good adjustment of these with greater number of close friends and interaction with them (Paintal 1976 : 101-109).

Regarding the health conditions of retirees there are few studies highlighting the common ailments of the retiree in India (Joshi 1971 : 64068, Bharat Pensioners' Samaj 1971).

There is a paucity of studies on family and social relationships of the retirees. The studies so far conducted explain that aged males play no role in maintaining their families (Soodan 1972 : 50-52), and that the retirees' flexible approach to family life enable them to feel satisfied and well-adjusted in their relation with others (Bhatia 1983 : 131). One study concerned with the aged people in a village observes that the older are not treated as isolated units and that they are regarded as part and parcel of the family and that they continue to discharge their responsibility in carrying towards the caste traditions (Marula Siddaiah : 1972).

There is one study related to work and activity levels of the retirees in India. It demonstrates that an overwhelming proportion of the retirees prefer to continue the activities they pursued before retirement, and an insignificant proportion evinced no interest in these activities but almost fifty percent of them evinced keen interest in hobbies (Sharma 1971 : 76-77).

Studies on post-retirement problems

Studies on the problems of the retirees in India can be counted on finger tips. One of them dealing with the general problems of the retirees explains that the general problems of the retirees in India cluster around pension, family life, proximity of friends, anxiety and security (Deoras and Janabandhu 1979) and that the most frequently cited problems are related to income (Desai and Naik 1970).

There are only a few researches on the psychological problems of the retirees in India. One of them explains that mental illness increases among the retirees as the retirees advance in their age (Rao & Malathi 1972 : 319-332). On the contrary another study depicts that the retirees are free from socio-psychological problems because the young are very understanding of the problems of the retirees and treat their old parents with warmth and affection (Desai and Niak 1970). Another study observes that the retirees are called to cope with the changing values and life-styles in order to ascertain their position in the society (Kalish & Moriwak 1973 : 187-209.

Investigations which probed into the economic problems of the old people in some villages of India highlink higher incidence of dependency of high age groups among the old persons. The main causes of dependency include incapacitation and disabilities among the aged. The findings reveal that half of the aged population was happy with its lot. The proportion of the unhappy aged was higher among the female respondents than the males (Purohit and Sharma 1972 : 71-83). Another study points out that because of the present cost of living and rate of inflation many of the elderly people in India are receiving income that is inadequate to meet their basic economic wants (Malik 1980 : 298-303). Some studies observed that the socio-economic development of the aged population is not adequate to meet the needs of the aged persons in India (Bhattacharjee 1982 : 41-48).

There are only a few studies which deal with the problems of women retirees in India. Two of them write that in India there were 318.2 millions of people in 1981 among whom 46 millions were engaged in economic activities and out of the total workers in the modern sector, which included nurses, teachers, clerks, typists, doctors and so on, 19.9 per cent were women (Radha Devi 1983), and that in the near future there will be a growing numbers of retired women whose problems will be different in many aspects from those of the retired men (Ranade & Ramachandran 1970 : 5). Some more studies reveal the differential problems of adjustment of aged men and women to their day-to-day activities. (Dayal & Dhasandraiah 1983, Menachery 1983, 1984,1985).

A few studies focusing their attention on the problem of retired migrants in India speak of specific problems and difficulties of retirees who settled permanently in cosmopolitan cities like Bangalore, Bombay and New Delhi (Kalish & Moriwak 1973, Preme 1984 : 274-285).

Methodology 3

This chapter describes the design of the study which attempts to discover the reasons behind the similarities and differences in the economic, social, religious, recreational and other types of adjustment and problems of the gazetted and non-gazetted retirees. The chapter provides an overview of the way the research population was chosen and located, a discussion of the combined techniques used for collecting the data and a description of the method of analyzing the data.

The chapter shows that the sample population for the present enquiry comprises 200 retirees of whom 95 are gazetted and males, and 5 are gazetted and females, and 95 are non-gazetted and males and 5 are non-gazetted and females. The primary tool of data collection is a schedule with 11 parts and 23.6 questions. The information gathered with the help of the schedule was supplemented by information obtained through informal discussions, observation, case studies and individual biographies. The analysis was presented by means of two-way tables. Standard normal probability tests and Chi-square tests were employed to know the significant differences between the two large sample means and to understand the degree of independence of two attributes respectively.

SAMPLING DESIGN OF THE STUDY

Universe of the study

According to the 1981 Census, Tirupati has a population of 115,292 of which 32,900 are workers and 82,392 are non-workers. Of the 32,900 workers, 22,793 are employees and the remaining 10,207 are agricultural labourers and others. Among the employees, 9,732 are gazetted officers and 13,061 are non-gazetted officers. Gazetted officers are those who are engineers, doctors, section officers, accounts officers, lecturers, professors and ranks of equivalent or above these cadres. On the other hand, the non-gazetted officers are the employees who are just below the above mentioned cadres and whose jobs are of normally clerical nature.

The non-workers include the retired employees also. None of the Census records give the number of retired employees in Tirupati. To overcome this difficulty, a list of retired people in Tirupati was prepared to have a clear idea of the total population of the retirees. The list included several details like name, address, age, sex, official status, employer, amount of pension, date of employment, and date of retirement of every employer. The treasury office, banks, administrative office of the temples of Tirumala and Tirupati known as Tirumala–Tirupati Devasthanams (T.T.D.), and associations of retired persons are approached to obtain the lists of retired employees. The details required are perfectly traceable. The retirees worked in different departments such as education, medical, engineering, electricity, municipality, temple administration, revenue, banks, industries, police and transport. They belong to gazetted and the non-gazetted categories. Of the 2,138 retirees, 853 are gazetted retirees and the remaining 1285 are the non-gazetted retirees. This total retirees population in Tirupati has become the universe of the present study.

Table-1 shows the percentage distribution of the retired employees in Tirupati according to their gazetted and non-gazetted status and the department in which they worked. The table clearly shows the numerical preponderance of the non-gazetted over the gazetted retirees. Further, the largest retirees are from the administrative service of the Tirumala Tirupati Devasthanams (T.T.D.).

Sample chosen for the study

The sampling design used for the study is the Stratified Random Sampling with an individual as a sampling unit.

Using random numbers, a ten percent sample has been arrived at by picking out a sample of 200 respondents from the lists, 100 from the list of gazetted retirees and 100 from the non-gazetted retirees. This sample included 5 gazetted and 5 non-gazetted women retirees also. Table-2 shows the percentage distribution of the sample of retired employees chosen according to the department in which they worked.

Table 1. Percentage Distribution of the Retired Population in Tirupati According to the Department in which they worked

Department	Retired employees		Total
	Gazetted	Non-Gazetted	
T.T.D (Tirumala Tirupati Devasthanams)	254	394	648 (30.31)
Revenue	218	346	564 (26. 38)
Electricity	42	91	133 (6.23)
Transport	39	58	97 (4.53)
Industries	56	59	115 (5.38)
Railways	36	88	124 (5.80)
Police	12	45	57 (2.67)
Banks	33	28	61 (2.85)
Municipality	34	94	128 (5.99)
Education	83	41	124 (5.80)
Engineering	17	28	45 (2.10)
Medical	29	13	42 (1.96)
Total	853	1285	2138 (100.00)

Note : The percentages are shown in parentheses

Table 2. Percentage Distribution of the Retired Employees According to the Department in which they worked

Previous Organization	Retired employees		Total
	Gazetted	Non-Gazetted	
T.T.D. (Tirumala Tirupati Devasthanams)	22	23	45 (22.5)
Revenue	20	21	41 (20.5)
Electricity	9	10	19 (9.5)
Transport	5	6	11 (5.5)
Industries	7	6	13 (6.5)
Railways	5	7	12 (6.0)
Police	4	6	10 (5.0)
Banks	6	4	10 (5.0)
Municipality	8	10	18 (9.0)
Education	9	3	12 (6.0)
Engineering	2	3	5 (2.5)
Medical	3	1	4 (2.0)
Total	100	100	200 (100.0)

The table shows that nearly half of the number of respondents chosen for the study are from the T.T.D. (Tirumala Tirupati Devasthanams) and the Revenue Deparetment. T.T.D. is a big organization of temple administration in Tirupati. More than 6000 people are on its pay rolls ; obviously, employees from T.T.D. form bulk of the working and retired employees in Tirupati. Apart from the T.T.D., the Revenue Department is another big organization with hundreds of its employees. Therefore, the retirees from the T.T.D. and the Revenue Department form a larger part in the sample of respondents.

DATA GATHERING PROCESS

Techniques of data collection

Many techniques have been combined to get as extensive information as possible of the retirees chosen for the study.

The techniques employed are:

i. Filling in an interview schedule for each individual among the retirees;

ii. Observation , both participant and non-participant, as conditions permitted;

iii. Collection of case studies and recording of the biography of some retirees.

The use of the above mentioned combined techniques has helped not only in getting relevant data but also in acquiring certain information for deeper understanding of the social and cultural aspects of the retired employees chosen for the present enquiry.

Collection of data

The retirees are residing in different municipal wards. Almost 25 percent of the retirees are living in the recently constructed colonies meant for the gazetted and non-gazetted employees. It took almost a fortnight to locate the houses of the retirees selected for the present study.

After locating the houses of the respondents, the investigator visited the house of every respondent and spent half an hour to one hour just to get acquainted with the people. These initial contacts were used to inform the subjects about the nature of the study and to give some indications as to the type of information they might have to provide. These preliminary procedures and a peripheral identification constituted much to obtaining a good entry and rapport in the field. Almost five months were spent in this regard.

However, only the daytime was utilized for establishing the rapport with the respondents. At home, the nighttime was successfully utilized for preparing an interview schedule. The schedule included eleven parts. Part-1 dealt with the personal background of retirees. It included items likes name, address, age, date of birth, sex, religion, case, tribe, languages known, education, date of employment, date of retirement, age at retirement, and household composition. Part-2 embraced questions related to the daily routine, household composition and living arrangements of the retirees. Part-3 contained questions concerned with the concept of retirement, mandatory retirement and attitudes toward compulsory retirement. Some of the questions highlight how retirement is treated as an institutionalized event in one's life. Parts-4 to 7 included questions related to planning for retirement, problems at the time of retirement, problems after retirement and personal satisfaction on retirement.

Part-8 consisted of questions dealing with the economic adjustment in retired life. In this context, questions were formed to elicit information on annual income and expenditure, savings and property, control over finances and property, adequacy or inadequacy of income, modes of economic adjustment in terms of reduction of needs, judicious utilization of savings and financial help from children and relatives. In addition, questions on attitudes toward economic support obtained from children, friends and relatives were also included.

Part-9 dealt with the family life of the retirees. The questions in this regard were designed to get information on the preferences of the retirees to small or a big family, conditions and problems of those retirees who are living alone because of the death, separation or long absence of spouse, problems and difficulties of these retirees who have no children, or whose children are living at different places, and the problems of those retirees who are living along with their children and who are living in a joint family. Apart from dealing with these aspects of the family life of the retirees, the questions also considered other aspects of domestic life of the retirees such as authority and influence, financial control and management, consultation on family matters, key role in keeping up the interests of the family, control over children, old age dependency, and inter-personal and inter-generational relations.

Part-10 was concerned with the health problems of the retirees. It included questions related to present state of health, health and social values, feelings about illness, and support received from relatives and friends during times of ill health. Part-II dealt with the socio-psychological problems of the retirees. It included questions related to perception of old age status, religious problems of the aged, problems related to leisure time activities, problem of social isolation and loneliness and ambitions in old age.

Altogether all the eleven parts of the schedule embraced 280 questions. The schedule was then administered among ten retirees, five each from the gazetted and non-gazetted categories, to test its validity and reliability. The pre-testing of the schedule proved that some questions were to be modified, a number of questions were to be restricted, certain questions were to be deleted and a few questions were to be replaced by more relevant ones. After carrying on all these changes, the schedule came to have 234 questions. For preparing, pre-testing and standardizing the schedule besides establishing a good rapport with the retirees it took almost five months for the investigator

The standardized schedule included direct, indirect, probing, filtered, closed, open-ended and multiple choice questions. Probing questions were framed to collect information on age. Indirect questions were formed to collect details on socio-economic items. Direct, indirect and probing questions were used to collect data on attitudes of the respondents. Though the questions were printed in English they were asked in Telugu also depending upon the convenience of the respondents. Greater relevance was placed on free and informal interviews.

The canvassing of the schedule took almost one year. Most of the retirees were to be personally interviewed more than once. Some difficulties were faced while interviewing both the gazetted and non-gazetted retirees.

One of the problems was that a few retirees leading an energetic life were so much pre-occupied with their work that neither in the morning nor in the afternoon, they were available at random. So, the interview was to be conducted whenever they were available. Often, a person had to be visited more than a dozen times to complete one interview because he was unable to spare enough time in one sitting.

Another problem encountered in the field was that some of the respondents were reluctant to give information on problems of their family life. It was only after giving them repeated assurances that strict anonymity would be maintained with regard to the information provided by them, they could give information on the delicate issues concerning their personal and family life.

A third problem encountered in the field was related to the income and expenditure besides the family budgets of the retirees. Some informants from non-gazetted ranks exaggerated their family budgets, while others gave scanty information about their family budgets. To solve this problem, details about the total expenditure incurred on various items during the previous years were asked first, then details of the total income were asked. An average of these two was taken as the actual income of the respondent's family.

A different problem was that nearly thirty percent of the informants asked that in what way the information solicited from them would be use full. They were convinced that it would be useful not only for the thesis but also for the planners and administrators who are concerned with the welfare programmmes of the aged populance.

Altogether a different problem was faced while interviewing some of the retired employees. Respondents aged more than 65 felt that interviewing was laborious process to them. However, topics of their interest were discussed now and then to relieve them from the labour of answering the questions. Despite all these problems, field work was completed successfully.

Apart from obtaining much information by means of a schedule, valuable information on the attitudes and problems of respondents has been elicited through informal conversations. The schedule was a necessity as it provided a frame of reference to proceed on. The informal discussions prevented being over bound by the frame of reference. The necessary information that used to come out from the informal discussions was noted immediately after leaving the company of the retirees. Neighbours, friends and relatives of the respondents also provided a great deal of background information of the retirees.

Collection of data through the schedule was also supplemented by participant and non-participant observation. The investigator could participate in a number of functions and festivals whenever an invitation was extended by the respondents. Through voluntary help like bringing medicines, providing some sacred books wanted by the retirees, transmitting a message from the retirees to some of their friends, relatives, or religious mentors, the investigator could win the hearts of some of the respondents and obtain valuable information of social, economic and psychological problems of the retirees. Though participant observation, required information on many aspects of life of the retirees could be recorded.

Concrete case histories and biographies of some selected respondents were also collected. Requisite number of cases were collected from different individuals which were subject to careful scrutiny before drawing conclusions.

Regarding the total time requirement, in the beginning it was planned to gather data through a schedule, observation and personal discussions for a continuous period of one year. But in practice the period had to be extended for a few more months. As some respondents had fallen sick either intermittently or continuously for a long time, the data could not be collected during the planned period. The field work was continued for one year and four months. Almost five months were spent to have initial contact with the respondents to prepare, pre-test and standardize the schedule. Altogether field work continued for one year and nine months from March 1987 to December 1988.

ANALYSIS OF DATA

Variables under study

The variables chosen for the present study are social status, financial position, residence, age, sex, occupation, health, family composition, languages known, official position (before retirement), religion, economic adjustment, socio-psychological attitudes, opinions on the event of retirement, personal satisfaction on retirement, employment of retired people, status in the family and society, and relationships with family members and daily activities.

Analysis of aspects of retirement

While formulating the research design, the whole study was divided into eleven chapters covering five major aspects of retirement:

i. Economic adjustment

ii. Social adjustment

iii. Health

iv. Socio-psychological conditions and

v. Religious activities

The analysis of economic adjustment gives a comparative picture of the economic conditions and problems of the gazetted and non-gazetted retirees in terms of their income, expenditure, distribution of savings and property and adequacy or inadequacy of income and shows how the retirees from the gazetted and non-gazetted categories cope with the post-retirement economic deprivations and other related economic matters. The analysis presents different profiles of the respondents to represent patterns of economic adjustment.

The analysis of social adjustment brings out the similarities and differences with regard to the patterns of adjustment of the gazetted and non-gazetted retirees within their families.

The analysis pertaining to health conditions of the retirees presents an overall picture of the health problems faced by the retirees and shows how health conditions alter the lives of the retirees and how the gazetted and non-gazetted retirees tackle the situations in similar and different ways.

The analysis of the socio-psychological conditions and religious activities of the retirees presents the similarities and differences related to the perception of old age status, religious problems of the retirees, problems related to leisure time activities of the retirees, problems of social isolation and loneliness among some retirees.

The responses have been arranged in two-way frequency tables according to different variables under study. These tables have been particularly useful in the analysis of respondents' attitudes, opinion and behavioural orientation concerning the self in different life situations.

Reliance has also been placed on the use of case studies in the analysis and presentation of field-data. The cases have been used to illustrate specific aspects and dimensions of the respondent's life where general observations failed to bring out the point very clearly. The case approach has further been applied in the analysis to explain the presence of certain unique features in the retired employee's life. This has made it possible to bring together the multiplicity of factors related to the approach, orientations or behaviour of individual respondents in their relationship with others and to their perception of the situation in which they find themselves.

Some of the cases brought out the latent personality factors of the retirees which it was not possible to get otherwise.

Statistical techniques used for the analysis

The following statistical tools were applied in analysing the sample data:

a. **Arithmetic Mean:**

It is given by

$$\overline{X} = \left[\frac{\Sigma fx}{N}\right]$$

(r x s) Contingency table

A\B	B_1	B_2	-----	B_s	Total
A_1	O_{11}	O_{12}	-----	O_{1s}	(A_1)
A_2	O_{21}	O_{22}	-----	O_{2s}	(A_2)
.					
.					
.					
.					
.					
A_r	O_{r1}	O_{r2}	-----	O_{rs}	A_r
Total	(B_1)	(B_2)	-----	(B_s)	N

Where , x's are mid values of classes

f's are their corresponding frequencies

N is the Total frequency

Σfx is the sum of products of mid values of classes and their corresponding frequencies.

b. Standard normal probability test (Z- Test)

This test is used for knowing the significant difference between two large sample means.

Suppose $\overline{X}_1$ and $\overline{X}_2$ are arithmetic means of two large samples of sizes n-1 and n-2 respectively. Also let S_1^2 and S_2^2 denote the variance of these two samples respectively. To test the significance of difference between these two sample means, the null hypotheses may be stated as:

Ho: There is no significant difference between the two sample arithmetic means.

To test the null hypothesis, the Z- test statistic is given by

$$Z = \frac{\overline{X}_1 - \overline{X}_2}{\sqrt{\left[\frac{S_1^2}{n_1} + \frac{S_2^2}{n_2}\right]}}$$

The calculated value of Z can be compared with either 1.96 or 2. 58 and the inference can be drawn accordingly. If Z cal 1.96 or Z cal 2.58 then Ho may be rejected either at 5% level or at 1% level of significance; otherwise Ho may be accepted.

c. Chi- square Test (X^2 – test) for Independence of Two Attributes

Suppose A and B are any two attributes with 'r' and 's' sub-classes respectively. Write the sub-classes as A1, A2 ....Ar for attribute 'A' and B1, B2........Bs for attribute 'B'. The (r x s) contingency table may be written as follows:

Where Oij = The observed cell frequency In the (I, j)th cell

i = 1,2,..........r

j = 1,2........s

(A,i) = Row total under A, i

(B,j) = Column total under B, j

N = Total frequency

The corresponding expected frequencies can be calculated by writing the following formula:

$$E_{ij} = \frac{(Ai)\ (Bj)}{N}$$ = The expected frequency corresponds to oij

To test the independence of two attributes, the null hypothesis may be stated as:

Ho: The given two attributes are independent to each other.

OR

There is no association between two attributes.

To test the Ho, the X2 – test statistic is given by :

$$X^2 = \sum \frac{(Oij - Eij)^2}{Eij}$$

The calculated value of X^2 can be compared with its critical value for [(r-1) (s-1)] degrees of freedom either at 5% level or at 1% level of significance and the inference can be drawn accordingly.

Tirupati : The Town and its People

4

This chapter examines the demographic features, residential areas, available resources and work places of the retirees, the subjects of this study, by looking at the larger community in which they are located, i.e., the pilgrim town of Tirupati, whose people, organization, culture and resources provide the facilitations or constraints for the diverse activities of the employees at every stage of their life, especially in their retired life.

TRADITION AND MODERNITY

Population

Tirupati, a growing town revealing tradition as well as modernity, is located between 13° 38^{1} North Latitude and $79^{O}21^{1}$ East Longitude. Its tradition and modernity are inherent in its location at the foot hills of great sanctity, its function as a hub of transportation and communication, the diversity of its economic base, its social heterogeneity and its long standing image as a pilgrim center par excellence. Tirupati is acclaimed as the `Vatican of India'.

Tirupati was a large village before it was declared a municipal town in the year 1886. Its population was 14,242 in 1891. Within a period of less than century between 1891 and 1981 its population has crossed 1,00,000 mark.

Table – 3 shows the population and the decennial growth rates of the population of Tirupati from 1891 to 1981. In a span of 60 years between 1901 and 1961 the population became doubled but it took only a decade between 1961 and 1971 for another doubling of population. In this regard, migration has played a dominant role.

The growth rate of the population remained at less than one per cent from 1901 to 1941 in Tirupati because of high mortality. However, as the health and medical facilities in the form of public

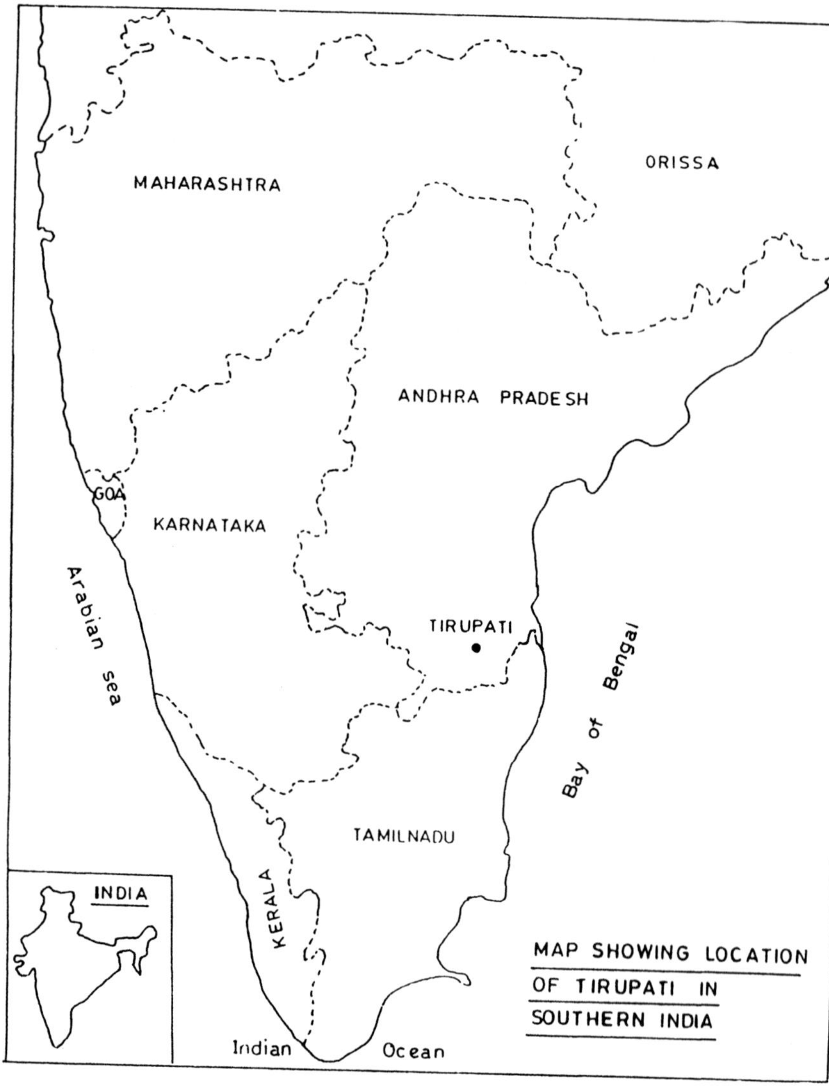

MAP SHOWING LOCATION OF TIRUPATI IN SOUTHERN INDIA

and private hospitals, dispensaries and nursing homes have increased since 1951, the mortality rate has shown a downward trend from 1955 onwards. This is also one of the dominant reasons for the high growth rate of population between 1951 and 1961.

Table 3. Population of Tirupati between 1881 and 1981 with Decadal Variations and Percentage Decade Variation

Year	Population	Decade Variation	%Decade Variation
1981	13,292	—	—
1891	14,242	+950	+7.15
1901	15,485	+1243	+8.73
1911	16,701	+1216	+7.85
1921	17,434	+733	+4.39
1931	19,138	+1704	+9.77
1941	20,143	+1005	+5.25
1951	25,207	+5064	+25.14
1961	35,845	+10638	+42.20
1971	65,843	+29998	+83.68
1981	1,15,292	+49449	+75.10

However, since 1961, migration has played an important role for the rapid growth rate of population in Tirupati. The expansion of the temple administration institutions, banks, commercial centers and industries, besides expansion of transport and communication facilities have provided several employment opportunities by which migration has become more to the town during the decade 1961-1971 and still more during 1971-1981 and afterwards.

Social diversity

The population of the town and its suburbs is not homogeneous. There are about 38 ethnic groups in the town and its suburbs of whom 35 are castes and 3 are tribes. Out of the 35 castes, 9 belong to Forward Castes, 24 belong to the Backward Classes, and 2 belong to the Scheduled Castes. Apart from these caste and tribal groups, there are Muslims, Christians, Jains, Buddhists and Sikhs.

The nine Forward Caste groups are the Brahmin (priest), the Komati (traders), the Reddi (agriculturists), the Kamma (agriculturists), the Balija (traders), the Raju (agriculturists and rulers), the Mudaliar (agriculturists), the Karanam (accountants) and the velama (agriculturists).

The castes belonging to the Backward Classes are the Golla (shephered), the Gandla (oil-monger), the Bondili (rulers), the Kummari (potters), the Jangam (Saivite-priests), the Sattadas (Srivaishnava priests), the Bestha (fishermen), the Kamsali (smiths), the Ediga (toddy-tappers), the Vodde (earth-workers), the Muttaracha (fishermen), the Palli (fisherfolk), the Sale (weavers), the Thogata (weavers), the Patnool-sale (weavers), the Kaikola (weavers), the Agaru (labourers), the Perika (traders), the Naikar (agriculturists), the Boya (labourers), the Pitchchiguntla (bards), the Dasari (nomadic traders), the Chakali (Washermen) and the Mangali (Barbers).

The Scheduled Castes living in Tirupati are the Mala (labourers) and the Madiga (leather-workers). Of the three tribes, while the Yanadi (food-gatherers) and Nakkala (fox-eaters) are Scheduled Tribes, the Yarukala (basket-weavers) is an Ex-Criminal or a Denotified Tribe.

Table–4 shows the distribution of the population of Tirupati by religion in the years 1931, 1971 and 1981. It is clear from the table that a vast majority of the population in all the three census years belong to the Hindu religion. But it is interesting to note the existence of Sikhs, Muslims, Christians, Jains and Buddhists in the list.

Physical diversity

The physical herterogeneity in terms of its functional diversity shows how there are specific ecological areas within the town limits. There is the `bazaar area' situated around the main thoroughfare of the town. The population of this area is approximately 18,000 and an aged population of a hundred can be seen in this area. The Vaisyas (traders) are seen in more numbers in this area as their business establishments are situated in this area. Even the Balijas, Reddis and Kammas are owning a few commercial enterprises in this area. It is the crucible of the commercial enterprises and beehive of business activity as most of the nationalized banks, revenue office, treasury office, shops, emporia, hotels, lodges, etc., are situated in this 'bazaar area'.

Table 4. Distribution of Population of Tirupati by Religion

Year	Population by religion							Total
	Hindus	Sikhs	Muslims	Christians	Jains	Buddhists	Others	
1931	17,719 (92.58)	–	1,404 (7.34)	6 (0.03)	9 (0.05)	–	–	19,138
1971	60,566 (91.99)	–	4,548 (6.91)	667 (1.01)	–	–	52 (0.09)	65,843
1981	105.695 (91.67)	37 (0.03)	7,364 (7.25)	1069 (0.93)	122 (0.10)	5 (0.02)	–	115,292

SOURCE : 1. Census of India 1981, Series-2 A.P. Paper 1 of 1985

2. Census Handbook 1951, Chittoor District.

The 'residential-cum-bazaar area' is found in the places adjoining the 'bazaar area'. This can be termed as a transitional area because this area is composed and several residential households besides several shops and a variety of commercial establishments. The population of this area is approximately around 25,000 and an aged population of about 300 can be seen here. Those people whose traditional occupation is trade and who have also served in some organizations are seen in these places.

About ten 'residential areas' are scattered throughout the town haphazardly. These areas are clusters of households distributed randomly in the main centers of the town. A population of about 30,000 stay in these residential areas. These are the places which account for nearly sixty percent of the retiree population in the town.

The 'educational area' is situated at the western end of the town. It comprises of institutions of higher education, where graduate courses are taught in Degree Colleges and post-graduate courses are taught in the university colleges. The aged are less in number in this area. Mostly young population is seen in this area. About 18,000 people live in this area.

The `industrial-cum–working men area' is situated outside the municipal limits at the eastern end of the town. This area contains mostly workers living nearby with very less number of aged population. The population of this area is around 12,000.

There are eleven slums where the poorer sections of the population live. The non-gazetted employees other than clerks and administrative assistants and even some people of middle level ranks in the non-gazetted category of retired employees live in the slums. The populations of this slums is approximately 25,000.

The `peripheral area' includes residential clusters, known as colonies in local parlance. Nearly 60 percent of the town's retired employees live in these residential clusters because the latter contain good air and ventilation and are free from noice pollution. The residential clusters contain shops, community halls, schools and marriage halls besides a number of houses. Around 12,000 people live in these areas.

RESOURCES OF THE TOWN

Changes in the ecological areas

The doubling of population after 1961 has played a great role in getting the town expanded vastly. The town wears a new look as a result of the expansion. Expansion of commercial enterprises, growth of population mostly by in-migration, industrial development and educational development have all shaped the ecological areas.

A virtual housing boom has changed the residential scene in the town. House building activity has been encouraged, by the government and other institutions of work. Financial loans have been made feasible to many sections of the people as part of the encouragement. As a result, there has been a steep increase in the number of individual houses and residential colonies. Several people have gone for new places to build their houses and as a result the periphery of the town got extended. Almost four decades ago only the thatched houses, tiled houses, huts and terraced buildings formed the skyline. As new residential buildings, shopping complexes and such other high-rise structures started coming up, the skyline of the town has changed.

In the last twenty years, several industries have come up at the eastern periphery of the town. A huge Carriage Repair Workshop of the Indian Railways is under construction.

Tirupati has become an important center of transport and communication network. It is accessible by rail, road and air from different towns and cities in India. The traffic in the town as a result of the expansion has grown very much. The in-bound traffic has grown so much that the main roads and the connecting roads are nowhere wide enough to meet the in-bound traffic expansion. The out-bound traffic as a result of Tirupati being connected to various important villages, towns and cities, has also grown. New by–pass roads connecting the peripheries of Tirupati have been laid to meet the out-bound traffic. Large number of commercial and unprecedented pilgrim influx in the past twenty years have influenced the municipality to lay new roads and create traffic networks.

In the past two decades work places have also grown in their number and size. New educational institutions, new offices and new commercial centers under private management have started coming up in these places.

Medical and health services were previously provided by the government hospital in the town. To meet the growing needs of the town several private nursing homes and consulting clinics have been established in the past twenty-five years. A super-specialities hospital is coming up near the existing general hospital where new areas of specialities in medical science are going to be introduced.

The emergence of Tirupati as one of the leading religious centers in India is entirely due to the location of important temples such as those of Govindarajaswami, Kodandaramaswami and Kapileswaraswami within it and the location of the temple of Lord Venkateswara at Tirumala. Most of the pilgrims who visit Tirumala in large numbers every day also visit the temples in Tirupati, otherwise the pilgrimage is not supposed to be complete.

As the population of Tirupati contains Christians and Muslims, a few mosques and churches are seen in the town.

The consequences of the expansion of Tirupati are also seen on the negative side of the quality of life. The growing atmospherical pollution as a result of industrial expansion and pilgrim influx, added to the problems of the aged in the town.

The privacy of the retirees before expansion gave them mental tranquility. The uncomfortable weather has created unease among the aged in the town. This is one of the reasons why a good number of the aged live in the 'peripheral area' of the town.

The high rate of pilgrim influx is another menace to the aged population because it has become a source of contamination in many areas.

As a result of the expansion in population, there is a great effect on the general price index going up causing financial hardship to the aged.

These are the general problems faced by the aged populace as a result of the multi-faceted growth of the town.

RETIRED EMPLOYEES

Retirees in general

The retired employees numbering more than 2000 are

concentrated in specific areas, mostly in the peripheral are as (areas) in the town. In several other areas of the town also, the aged employees are seen but in less number. Most of the employees want to lead a peaceful retired life in the colonies and residential clusters located in the 'peripheral area' of the town. There are no circumscribed residential places which are specifically meant for the gazetted and non-gazetted retirees. Even though there is a colony called N.G.O's Colony, many gazetted retirees are also living in this colony.

The retired employees are aged 58 years and above. Among the retired employees those aged between 58 and 63 years comprise more than 50 percent, those aged between 64 and 68 years comprise 40 per cent and the rest are those aged 69 years and above.

The social status of the aged employees in the town gives mixed picture. A good number of the retired population belong to the Forward Castes. A quarter of the total number of aged employees belong to the Backward Classes and the rest belong to the Scheduled Castes and Scheduled Tribes. About 3 to 5 percent of the employees come from the Christian and Muslim communities.

The educational status of the gazetted and the non-gazetted retirees is different. By virtue of their official status the gazetted are more in number with higher educational qualifications than the non-gazetted. There are almost no gazetted retirees whose education has stopped at primary or secondary levels. Nearly three-fourths of the gazetted retirees have college level educational status and the rest hold other degrees and diplomas with technical background. Among the non-gazetted retirees less than fifty percent account for college level education and the rest come from primary, secondary and other educational backgrounds with technical qualifications.

The cultural activities of the retirees in the town include participation in religious discourses, attendance at devotional music concerts and recitation of sacred texts. The recreational activities of the retirees include seeing the cinemas, dramas and video films, playing chess, badminton and other games, and enacting traditional and modern plays. More than fifty percent of the retired employees participate in traditional cultural activities like religious discourses, devotional music, programmes and recitial of sacred texts. Besides, they also attend dance, drama and music centers such as

Table 5. Distribution of the sample of Retirees according to their Age

S. No.	Age Groups (in years)	Retirees Gazetted	Retirees Non-Gazetted	Total
1.	55-60	41	49	90 (45%)
2.	61-55	34	20	54 (27%)
3.	66-70	19	23	42 (21%)
4.	71 and above	6	8	14 (7%)
	Total	100	100	200 (100%)

Thyagaraja Mandapam and Annamacharya Kalamandiram.

Retirees selected for the study

The subjects selected for the present study are 200 in number of whom 100 are gazetted retired employees and 100 are non-gazetted retired employees. Among these retirees, 123 live in the 'residential areas'of the town and 47 live in the 'peripheral area' and the rest in other areas of the town which include slums, 'residential-cum-bazaar areas' and 'industrial–cum-working men area'.

Table–5 gives the distribution of the Retired Employees according to their Age Status. Nearly half the number of the retirees are in the age group of 50-60 years.

The table reveals that there is a pattern of semblance in age between the gazetted and non-gazetted, as the age of superannuation is 58 years in State service and 60 years in Central Service for both the categories. Further, it also shows that there is no correspondence between the age-status and official status.

Table-6 shows the distribution of the retired employees according to their marital status.

The table shows that a vast majority from both the gazetted and non-gazetted categories are married. Three retirees were not married and three were widowed. Three percent from both the categories belong to the unmarried group which is an insignificant number.

Table 6. Distribution of the Retirees according to their Marital Status

S. No.	Marital status	Retirees employees		Total
		Gazetted	Non-Gazetted	
1.	Married	96	98	194 (97%)
2.	Unmarried	2	1	3 (1.5%)
3.	Widowed	2	1	3 (1.5%)
	Total	100	100	200 (100%)

Table-7 shows the distribution of the retirees by their educational status.

A vast majority of the gazetted retires have college education as against the non-gaetted retirees because by virtue of their position the minmum educational qualification for a gazetted officer is a college degree. Nearly one- eight of the total retirees who come from technical side hold degrees, diplomas and certificates from technology institutions.

The sample respondents for the present study come from different social backgrounds. Table-8 shows the distribution of the retirees according to their ethnic status. The retirees are from the Forward Castes, Backward Classes, Scheduled Castes and Scheduled Tribes.

Table 7. Distribution of the Retirees according to their Educational Status

S. No.	Educational status	Retirees		Total
		Gazetted	Non-Gazetted	
1.	Primary	—	22	22 (11.0%)
2.	Secondary	—	68	68 (34.0%)
3.	Collegiate	78	7	85 (42.5%)
4.	Others	22	3	25 (12.5%)
	Total	100	100	200 (100.0%)

Table 8. Distribution of the Retirees according to their Ethnic Status

S. No.	Ethnic status	Retirees		Total
		Gazetted	Non-Gazetted	
1.	Forward Castes			
	a. Brahmin	10	7	17 (8.5%)
	b. Vaisya	9	9	18 (9%)
	c. Reddi	12	10	22 (11%)
	d. Balija	18	15	33 (16.5%)
	e. Kamma	11	13	24 (12%)
2.	Backward Class			
	a. Golla	13	7	20 (10%)
	b. Gandla	8	5	13 (6.5%)
	c. Bondili	3	2	5 (2.5%)
	d. Kamsali	3	3	6 (3%)
	e. Perike	—	2	2 (1%)
	f. Dasari	—	3	3 (1.5%)
	g. Mangali	—	2	2 (1%)
	h. Chakali	2	3	5 (2.5%)
3.	Scheduled Castes			
	a. Mala	6	7	13 (6.5%)
	b. Madiga	2	5	7 (3.5%)
4.	Scheduled Tribe			
	Yanadis	—	2	2 (1%)
5.	Others			
	a. Christians	1	2	3 (1.5%)
	b. Muslims	2	3	5 (2.5%)
	Total	100	100	200 (100%)

Table 9. Distribution of the Retirees according to the Languages known to them

S. No.	Languages known	Retirees		Total
		Gazetted	Non-Gazetted	
1.	English	100	87	184
2.	Telugu	93	97	190
3.	Tamil	21	26	47
4.	Hindi	34	28	62
5	Urdu	4	3	7

The table shows that more than half of the total number of respondents belong to the Forward castes which is in consonance with the fact that two-thirds of the total population in Tirupati belong to the Forward Caste groups.

Languages known

Table–9 shows the distribution of the retirees according to the languages known to them. Most of the retirees know at least two languages. Only a few retirees know more than two languages.

All gazetted retirees know English whereas only 84 percent of the non-gazetted retirees know English. Also more number of gazetted retirees speak more languages than the non-gazetted retirees.

Table–10 shows the distribution of the retirees according to their annual income.

The income given includes pension, interest on securities like bank deposits, Unit Trust of India, rents on houses and agricultural income.

Among the retired gazetted officers no one has a monthly income of Rs. 250 or less. Almost two-thirds of them have income ranging from Rs. 3,000 to Rs. 12,000 per annum, while one-third of them had income of more than Rs. 12,000 per annum. A majority of the non-gazetted retirees have a monthly income of less than Rs. 585.

Table 10. Distribution of the Retirees according to their Annual Income

S. No.	Annual Income in Rupees	Retirees		Total
		Gazetted	Non-Gazetted	
1.	3000 and below	—	23	23 (11.5%)
2.	3001 and 7000	24	44	68 (34%)
3.	7001 and 12000	41	23	64 (32%)
4.	12001 and above	35	10	45 (22.5%)
	Total	100	100	200 (100%)

The difference in income patterns between the gazetted and non-gazetted retirees is on par with that of the gazetted retirees. This can be attributed to the former's income from other sources like agriculture and house rents.

Table–11 shows the distributions of the retirees according to their religion.

Majority of the respondents are Hindus for the dominant religion in the town is Hindus. Christians and Muslims are also a part of Tirupati's population. That is why, Christians and Muslims from the retirees figured in the sample, even though they are very less in number.

Table 11. Distribution of the Retirees according to their Religion

S. No.	Religion	Retirees		Total
		Gazetted	Non-Gazetted	
1.	Hindus	97	95	192 (96%)
2.	Christians	1	2	3 (1.5%)g
3.	Muslims	2	3	5 (2.5%)
	Total	100	100	200 (100%)

Work and Retirement 5

Work has assumed a central position in the lives of the people, both with respect to time and to importance (Chown 1977 : 678). Meltzer noted that work took up a more significant part of the life of people over 45 (Meltzer 1965). Several cross-sectional studies suggest that workers nearing retirement may have higher attachment to their jobs than younger men. The schedule of the working man is so ordered that work becomes the center of all the day's activity. Work drives the activities of the employee. Maddox says that work has been a central life task and interest of American males as well as a source of income (Maddox 1968: 357). Even for females work has assumed in recent decades such varied rewards including income, opportunities for social interaction and a basis for self esteem (Chown 1977: 682), when work becomes the nucleus of a man's life, a change from it would predict certain negative consequences. This may not be true in the case of the employees whose psychological activities have other areas than work. Those who are working are found to have better score on morale, happiness and adjustment (Carp 1968). According to Kreps, work remains the measure of man; it provides the standard of judging his worth. Working man is driven by constant goals pertaining to his work during his working life (Kreps 1979: 13-18). In so doing time and other resources are spent judiciously.

Work occupies a vital place in developing social relationships. Working places give the opportunity for an employee to improve his contacts with people from different walks of life. The employees in the organization develop a sense of solidarity towards one another, being very conscious and cautious of the next man's position in the office and his promotional chances. This sort of an approach is developing at the working places. Retirement from this work means being deprived of such a milieu where he is enjoying a lot of privileges. Bromley aptly observes that the retiring person's problem is to find satisfactory ways of disengaging from employment without suffering economic hardship or emotional deprivations such as loneliness and boredom (Bromley 1966: 73).

Havighurst says that the development of urban technology has changed the nature of work career making it more complex (Havighurst 1973: 601). So the total pattern of jobs has undergone a major change, that is, the old simple jobs have given way for other occupations which need relatively early age of retirement. Sophistication has become a mandatory requirement in the industrial sector and other work places. 'Work division' is one factor which has taken its due place in the industrial advancement. So, occupations of different nature have evolved and as a result, there came at least two clear-cut sections in the industry: the class of labourers and the class of professionals. Though both are affected by retirement practice, it would mean different things to each one (Menachery 1987: 10). Consequently, there is a total reorganization of man's economic and social life. The new systems of production and consumption have created a distinctly new set of social roles based on altered relations between the worker and the tools he works with; in consequence, the manner and form in which he reaps the rewards of his labour has also changed (Orbach 1963: 391).

It is this 'working man' complex and its effect on one's life and attitudes that have made retirement a nighmare for many (Menachery 1987).

It is but natural and a cyclic process that work-life too begins and ends. Retirement denotes a formal ending of work-life (Gubrium k1976 : 198).

This chapter examines the work of the respondents before their retirement and the retirement from work as an event of socio-economic significance. The description deals with the traditional and modern meanings of the concept of work and the types of work in terms of labourers and professionals, white and blue collar workers, and, gazetted and non-gazetted employees. It also depicts the world of work in terms of schedule of work, learning to work, payment for work, and temperament, character, values, perceptions, and attitudes as moulded by workes. The depition shows how job is considered as a sine qua non for a male, how different types of work have created a diversity of statuses and roles for the respondents, and how the world of work gave the respondents specific types of work-personality.

The data relating to retirement of the respondents is analysed to understand the socio-economic implications of retirement. The analysis shows the differential patterns of age at retirement due to the differential policies of the State and Central Governments, the diversity of meanings with which the retirees understand the event of retirement, the dual opinions of the retirees with reference to compulsory retirement; the problems faced by the employees at the time of retirement and the opinion regarding re-employment. The analysis highlights the vacillating policies of the State Government from 1983 to 1986 with regard to reduction in retirement age and the consequent confusion created among the gazetted as well as the non-gazetted employees. The analysis also reveals how the gazetted feel about their retirement as deprivation of their status and authority and how the non-gazetted feel about their retirement as deprivation from life-sustaining activity.

Finally, the analysis shows how both the categories of employees take almost the same preparatory steps for retirement but face different socio-economic problems after their retirement. The living arrangement, levels of income and patterns of expenditure of both the categories of retirees reflect that the position of the gazetted is better than that of the non-gazetted retirees.

WORK

Concept of work

Webster's seventh New Collegiate Dictionary defines `work' as the labour, task, or duty that affords one his accustomed means of livelihood. Work, in the background of the current study, is mainly connected with livelihood activities. Elaborating this understanding work's main purpose, livelihood, remains the nucleus of other areas attached to work which serve psychological, occupational and recreational functions.

With a rapid growth of private and public organizations in India, paid employment as a mode of earning one's livelihood is becoming quite common in Indian society resulting into greater social and occupational mobility. In the last three decades in Tirupati the proportion of employees has grown to three times that of the employees in 1951. This increase in the percentage of employees is due to the growth of the temple organization, the establishment of several small, medium and large scale industries, the establishment of a large number of educational institutions, the opening of several commercial organizations, institutes and establishments and the expansion of health, communication, residential and hotel facilities in the last three decades.

Women's participation in work has grown after women's literacy started as a new trend. Women too took over management of many public domains. Employment in production or service organizations outside the home rewarded women with payment and other financial statuses.

But the traditional understanding of the concept of work is still holding its impact which says that work or job or employment is the quality of a male. This concept is an age old one which even in contemporary times has got validity to a larger extent. But at the same time, this phenomenon is fast changing in urban centres where work or job is no more associated or linked to males only. Even the segregation of works on the basis of sex is fast disappearing but for a few areas where the job is exclusively a male assigned one.

In olden days, that is yesteryears, job or employment was essential and it was immaterial where the place of job was. However, far may be the place of work one should go and complete it. These conditions were existing at a time when work was entirely a male-centered and a male-oriented one. In the process of getting a job one had to cross all barriers including language, geographical and cultural. Caste-oriented and caste-based jobs were the order of acquiring employment when the concept of work was traditional and conservative. Caste segregated works were the only classification methods. If a person has to acquire a job, the only option left to him was to choose a job allotted to his caste. This concept of work almost ruled over centuries and its ruins are still rampant in certain areas of work which is not questioned thoroughly.

The modern concept of work has entirely changed. Industrialisation resulted into a position that the nature of work had to change drastically. Earlier understanding and functions of work have undergone changes as more number of work places and varieties of work have started coming up to meet the needs of the modern society. But even at this stage, there is still belief that every male shall be employed.

Work related to administration occupied a large area where the white-collared employees with specialization in the area of administration started growing in number. Acquiring work in any part of the country of world has not changed from the past. This understanding and condition to acquire work is still alive in the world of work or employment. Caste-based works or employment have gone into oblivion in the transition into modern times. Industrial revolution has changed this concept completely.

Types of work

Work force in industries and offices can be broadly categorized into the following: professional and non-professional employees, skilled and unskilled labour. Further, the classification is understood as white collar and blue collar, gazetted and non-gazetted employees.

White collared employees are those whose work is exclusively associated with mental or intellectual exercises. Coming under this category are employees in offices, colleges, universities, revenue offices and other work places where work involves occupations which are not directly related to production or productive activities. On the other hand blue-collared workers are those whose job is directly linked to production and productive activity. Labourers are those whose activity and work orientation is completely manual and physical in nature. On the other hand, professionals are specialists in a particular field of activity in a factory or industry. Gazetted workers are those who are wrested with powers to execute a job and the non-gazetted are those who carry over the execution. This is broadly the difference between the gazetted and the non-gazetted officers.

The world of work

The average work-life period of a worker or an employee is 35 years. This is stipulated as a standard work-life period after taking into consideration the work conditions existing in different parts of the country. Different regions have different environmental and ecological conditions to which a particular institute of work conditions itself. The employees' pattern of work also differs from institution to institution. For example, the Central organizations like Posts and Telegraphs and Railways work for its employees and workers. These organizations again see that the cumulative work done by a particular employee and his pay are corresponding to each other and the employees' unions and associations monitor and vanguard these matters. One of the key thrusts of workers'

Table 12. Percentage Distribution of the Retirees according to the Types of Work they were doing during their Service Period

S.No.	Type of work	Number of Gazetted Retirees	Number of Non-gazetted Retirees	Total
1.	Professional	22	11	33 (16.5%)
2.	Non-professional	59	71	130 (65%)
3.	Neither of the above	19	18	37 (18.5%)
	Total	100	100	200 (100%)

unions and employees' associations are focused on the working conditions vis-à-vis the wages received.

Table-12 shows the percentage distribution of the retirees in terms of their professional and non-professional varieties of work. It is apparent from the table that nearly two-thirds of the total sample were non-professional in their work nature.

The predominance of non-professional employees in the above table is because of the fact that a majority of the sample respondents come from offices and other institutions which are administrative in nature. The employees who work in these offices are naturally non-professional. Professional people among the gazetted are twice that of the non-gazetted because of the fact that there are more gazetted retirees with professional background than the non-gazetted.

There is a third category of work which neither belongs to professional nor to non-professional. This is according to the retirees' own notion of work in which they served during their service period. These retirees are in near equal members in both the gazetted and non-gazetted categories.

Among the non-professional category of retirees there are more number of non-gazetted than the gazetted. This is because of the fact that in any office clerks and other ministerial staff members numerically dominate their super-ordinates, that is, the officers.

Table–13 shows the percentage distribution of the retirees according to their emigration pattern. The figures clearly show that

Table 13. Percentage Distribution of the Retirees according to their Emigration Pattern after Retirement

S.No.	Emigration Pattern	Number of Gazetted Retirees	Number of Non-gazetted Retirees	Total
1.	Worked elsewhere and emigrated to Tirupati after retirement	29	22	51 (25.5 %)
2.	Worked and settled in Tirupati after retirement	71	78	149 (74.5%)
	Total	100	100	200 (100%)

those who worked and settled in Tirupati after retirement are three times more than those who worked elsewhere and emigrated to Tirupati after retirement.

All those who worked and settled in Tirupati after retirement comprising 75 percent of the total number of respondents are domiciles of Tirupati or Chittoor District. Therefore, they preferred to settle in Tirupati itself. Among the remaining 25 percent of the retirees, 8 percent emigrated to Tirupati because Tirupati has recorded a tremendous growth and development in the recent past in many fields like education, commerce and industry. Another 7 percent of the retirees thought that Tirupati, the abode of Lord Venkateswara, gives them solace. About 6 percent emigrated to Tirupati because they could look after the farm they possess in the nearby villages. More than 4 percent emigrated to Tirupati for they could live amidst their relatives who live scattered in a number of places located around Tirupati and in Tirupati itself.

Work–personality which is comprised of the temperament, character, values, perception, attitudes and approaches, is a major factor in the working–man complex of the retirees. Adjustment to work situation which resulted in learning to work at the work places moulded the work personality. Different employees and workers at different levels learnt and acclimatized to their work situations differently. The attitudes of subordinates were moulded in the process of their adjustment with their super-ordinates and vice-versa.

This work–personality had an impact on the employees to such an extent that this was carried over to the later life of the employees and still further, that is, their retired life. Work and leisure stages of the life-cycle had been so emerging into new systems that these had become less significant as persons of retirement age moved in and out of the work–force.

RETIREMENT

Age at retirement

Table-14 shows the percentage distribution of the retirees according to their age at retirement. Only 9.5 percent of the officers retired when they completed 60 years, but 36 percent retired when they completed 55 years and 54.5 percent retired when they completed 58 years. The age of retirement of both the categories of employees is thus different. This is because of the vacillating policies of the State Government of Andhra Pradesh in respect of retirement age of its employees.

The prescribed age for retirement of the Government servants in the State of Andhra Pradesh was 58 years upto 1982. When the reigns of power were taken by the Telugu Desam Party from the Congress Party in the year 1983, the former reduced the retirement age of the government servants to 55 years. Again due to some political upheavals and the Supreme Court judgment on Andhra Pradesh Government's Retirement Order, the retirement age of the Government servants was enhanced to 58 years in the year

Table 14. Percentage Distribution of the Retireees according to their Age at Retirement

S.No.	Age at Retirement	Number of Gazetted Retirees	Number of Non-gazetted Retirees	Total
1.	55 years	31	41	72 (36%)
2.	58 years	60	49	109 (54.5%)
3.	60 years	9	10	19 (9.5%0
	Total	100	100	200(100%)

`t' value =1.815

1985. Because of this confused state, some employees had to retire at 55 years and some had to be reinstated later and again had to retire at 58 years. These changes brought in the retirement age of the State Government employees were not made applicable to the College and University teachers in the state of Andhra Pradesh. Therefore, the retirement age of the College and University teachers stands even to this day as 60 years.

Event of retirement

Retirement begins not exactly on the date of retirement for an older person. On the contrary it begins in a phased manner when an atmosphere starts building up at the work place which has connotation of retirement.

Many employees' associations arrange farewell functions to retirees as a mark of formal parting and respect. This is a crucial stage for an individual retiree both psychologically and materialistically. The very next day is of a different nature for an employee as there will be a drastic change in the all round activities and needs of the retiree. Quite some time before the older employee starts making all arrangement for retirement some of the employees' associations help the person have a somewhat successful retirement. So the functions and farewell parties arranged in favour of the retirees before retirement have a mixed impact on the retirees.

Table-15 shows the percentage distribution of the retirees according to their concept of the event of retirement. More number of the non-gazetted employees accept retirement as a specific stage in their life, while more number of the gazetted employees take retirement as withdrawal from most of the social and economic responsibilities of adult life.

Among those who considered their retirement as a specific stage in their life, the proportion of the non-gazetted is almost double that of the gazetted. On the contrary, among those who regarded retirement as withdrawal from most of the social and economic responsibilities of adult life, the proportion of the gazetted is more than one and a half times that of the non-gazetted. More gazetted than non-gazetted also felt retirement as an end of life-long career of an employee.

The above facts reveals that non-gazetted employees regarded

Table 15. Percentage Distribution of the Retireees according to their Concept of the Event of Retirement

S.No.	Event	Number of Gazetted Retirees	Number of Non-gazetted Retirees	Total
1.	A specific stage in the life of an individual	23	43	66(33%)
2.	Withdrawal from most of the social and economic responsibilities of adult life	50	31	81(40.5%)
3.	Life with free-time activities and leisurely pursuits as its main goals	17	22	39(19.5%)
4.	End of a life–long career as an employee	10	4	14(7%)
	Total	100	100	200(100%)

Chi-square value =13.7299 (significant at 1% level)

their job as only a life-sustaining activity but felt some amount of suppression and hence their relief at the time of retirement. On the other hand, the gazetted officers got accustomed to an aura of authority and felt a little deprived of their status after retirement and were withdrawn from social and other activities.

Opinion on compulsory retirement

Table–16 shows the percentage distribution of the retirees according to their opinion on compulsory retirement. Among the gazetted, only one-third in contrast with two thirds opine that compulsory retirement is necessary. On the contrary among the non-gazetted almost equal proportions of the retirees give positive and negative responses to compulsory retirement respectively.

Table 16. Percentage Distribution of the Retirees according to their Opinion on Compulsory Retirement

S.No.	Opinion	Number of Gazetted Retirees	Number of Non-gazetted Retirees	Total
1	Compulsory retirement eradicates unemployment and stagnation and gives an opportunity for younger generation to produce skills and potentialities	34	47	81 (40.5%)
2.	No to the above opinion	66	53	119 (59.5%)
	Total	100	100	200(100%)

Chi–square value = 3.5066 (Not significant)

A vast majority of the gazetted gave negative response to compulsory retirement because they think that it helps employment of younger generation. Among the non-gazetted retirees those who wished compulsory retirement and those who opposed compulsory retirement as a means of employment to the younger generation are almost equal in their numerical proportion. This is because the non-gazetted employee is in a state of dilemma whereby he himself is facing economic problems and the problem of employment of his children.

Preparation for retirement

The gazetted as well as the non-gazetted employees prepared themselves for retirement. An important preparation for retirement is owing a house. In this context either a new house is constructed or an old house is purchased to reside after retirement. Another important preparation for retirement is total repayment of loans or total clearance of retirees to clear off the loans or debts.

Table 17. Percentage Distribution of the Retirees according to their Living Arrangements in terms of Own House and Rented House

S.No.	Living Arrangements	Number of Gazetted Retirees	Number of Non-gazetted Retirees	Total
1.	Own house	87	64	151 (75.5%)
2.	Rented house	13	36	49 (24.5%)
	Total	100	100	200 (100%)

Chi- square value = 14.2994 (significant at 1% level)

Table–17 shows the distribution of the retirees according to their living arrangement as part of the preparatory steps taken for retirement. Maximum number of respondents lived in their own houses and the rest in rented houses.

The high incidence of residing in own houses is because of the personal wish to reside in own house by the time of retirement. Among those who are living in their own houses 57.6 percent are gazetted, 42.4 percent are non-gazetted. This directly reflects better economic status of the gazetted government servant.

A house to live in is the hope of any person and it is but natural that many have achieved this. Out of the 200 retired employees studied, 38 percent have either built or purchased a house prior to or immediately after retirement utilizing their provident fund and gratuity. To be specific, 39 percent of the retired non-gazetted officers come under this category.

Repayment of loans taken during their service is the next priority item preparatory to retirement. About 35 percent of the employees have done this using their retirement benefits and 17 percent of the retirees performed the marriages of their daughters. There is not much of a significant difference between retired gazetted officers and non-gzetted officers in this preparatory step. The facility of obtaining housing loans has helped some of the employees to construct and own houses. Earlier age at marriage of the older generation (retired employees) usually results in their having children who have grown up sufficiently either for employment or marriage by the time they retire. Hence there is no significant difference between the gazetted and non-gazetted retirees in the steps taken preparatory to retirement.

Opinion regarding re-employment

Table–18 shows the percentage distribution of the retirees according to their opinion regarding re-employment. Among the retirees more than half as against less than half were willing for re-employment.

The table reveals that more than two-thirds of the non-gazetted and more than one-third of the gazetted were willing for reemployment. On the contrary, less than one-third of the non-gazetted and far more than one-third of the gazetted were not willing for re-employment. This reflects the economic independence of the gazetted employees and the economic deprivation of the non-gazetted employees after retirement. This also proves the following hypothesis:

Financial constraints after retirement make the retired employee seek re-employment.

Problems faced at the time of retirement

The problems of the retired employees are related to loss of income besides expenditure incurred on children's marriage and employment. The problems were more in the retired gazetted

Table 18. Percentage Distribution of the Retirees according to their Opinion Regarding Re-employment

S.No.	Opinion	Number of Gazetted Retirees	Number of Non-gazetted Retirees	Total
1.	Take up re-employment	41	68	109 (54.5%)
2.	Do not take up	59	32	91 (45.5%)
	Total	100	100	200 (100%)

Chi-square value= 14.6991 (Significant at 1% level)

Table 19. Percentage Distribution of the Retirees according to their Level of Satisfaction with Life in general

S.No.	Level of satisfaction	Number of Gazetted Retirees	Number of Non-gazetted Retirees	Total
1.	Less satisfied with life and took immediate retirement	24	21	45 (22.5%)
2.	Satisfied and continued to work even after retirement	58	51	109 (54.5%)
3.	Indifferent	18	28	46 (23.0%)
	Total	100	1001	200 (100%)

officers than among the non-gazetted officers. Financial problems were absent among 1 percent of the retired non-gazetted officers as against 13 percent of the retired gazetted officers. This trend indicates the earlier trend of financial instability during service and after retirement of non-gazetted officers.

Work and retirement

Table–19 shows the percentage distribution of the retirees according to their level of satisfaction with life in general. The table clearly shows that there are a significant number of retirees who showed less satisfaction with life and took immediate retirement.

The table clearly shows that slightly more than half of the total respondents were satisfied with life in general and continued to work even after retirement. But nearly one-fourth of the total retirees were less satisfied with life and took immediate retirement which in turn proves the hypothesis H_1 which says:

H1: Employees who accept immediate retirement tend to show less satisfaction with life in general than do the employees who continue to work even after retirement.

Again nearly one-fourth of the retirees were not able to answer to this question about their level of satisfaction. They were neither less satisfied nor more satisfied.

Economic Adjustment 6

Economic plight is a very important factor in retired life, as a steep income fall is experienced as soon as a person attains age of superannuation. To an employee the main source of income is salary. But after retirement a person is faced with the basic problem of economic needs. It is seen in the contemporary times that the care towards the aged is on the increase, that is, providing a majority of the aged with basic physical amenities of life. This is a fairly world-wide situation. But in some advanced countries where the general living conditions of the people are much better than those of the people in India, the aged population is in bad financial condition. Speaking about the economic problems of the American aged, Hurlock observes: "Relatively, few elderly people have adequate income from investments to meet their needs; most must depend on economic aid from public or private sources such as government, churches, institutions, friends and relatives; while some do continue to work full or part-time, most do not earn enough to meet their needs."(Hurlock 1968:854).

Discussing the employment policy and maintenance of income for the aged in the American Society, Jaunita M. Kreps suggests that "the economic plight of today's aged is intensified by the shrinking number of job opportunities for workers in their late fifties and early sixties and by the pressure of early retirement. Attempt to formulate policy dealing with the position of the aged must, therefore, take into account both the immediate pattern of economy-wide unemployment, which penalizes the older worker and threatens the adequacy of his future retirement benefits, and the secular trend toward earlier retirement which makes it necessary to spread work-life earnings over a longer now working period (Kreps, 1966:136)

It is a known fact that a large section of India's population is living below the poverty level. The retired population is no less apart from this economic crisis. But the position of the retirees is much better than that of the general aged population. Soowdan, in a study of the aged in a North Indian State capital, stated that 80 percent of the aged belonged to the lower income group (Rs. 100 per month or below) which included 190 out of 312 aged with no independent income of their own (Soodan 1975:55). Employees who retired from organizations which provide pension facilities are better placed than the general aged population.

Even in advanced countries the economic conditions of the aged are in a bad state. The comparison of the incomes of the aged population with those of the total population in the United States indicates that poverty is more concentrated in the population aged over 65 yeas and above than the total population (Walther 1975:340-341). Similarly in Japan, 80 percent of the households whose heads are aged 65 years and over and less than 20 years belong to the lowest income group (Ministry of Health and Welfare 1978:61).

It is a paradoxical situation in India for an employee to reach the retirement age when the financial needs are at their height and more funds are needed for maintaining a family.

It is hightime for a retiree to have a sound financial position to achieve a better adjustment in his old age or post-retirement life.,

So it is relevant to study the economic life of the retirees and their relationship with economic and new-economic matters and to portray their perceptions and reactions with regard to the financial front.

This chapter examines the economic adjustment and the factors that are responsible for the adjustment of the 200 retirees. In this regard, it not only reveals the differential sources and patterns of income and patterns of expenditure of the selected respondents but also delineates the discretion of the aged regarding their properties, adequacy of income, and other financial problems faced by the retirees. Finally, it shows the pattern of economic adjustment of the respondents.

INCOME

Sources of income

The sources of income are different for different retirees. Nearly half of the retirees from both the categories depend upon the pension amount. But the other half supplement their income by other sources. The most important supplementary sources of income are house-rent, post-retirement jobs, agriculture, interest on savings and business. Sources may be put under one category, that is, business, as these categories are nothing but business activities.

As regards the monthly pension of the retirees, it was found that the pension is different for different gazetted and non-gazetted retirees. The ranges of pension vary between Rs. 400 and Rs. 1,400 for non-gazetted and between Rs. 1,500 to Rs. 1,800 for gazetted retirees. Those retirees whose pension scales are fixed before July 1986 draw a different range of pension. They are between Rs. 200 and Rs. 700 for non-gazetted and Rs. 750 and Rs. 1,500 for gazetted retirees.

Mr. R.S.N. Murthy, a retired Upper Division Clerk from Andhra Pradesh Government Service, says, "I get a pension of about Rs. 600 and other sources like interest on bank deposits and house rent and I live in my own house comfortably." Altogether this respondent gets an income around Rs. 1,700 a month which helps him in having a peaceful post-retirement life.

Table 20. Distribution of the Retirees according to their Sources of Income

S.No.	Source of Income	Number of Gazetted Retirees	Number of Non-gazetted Retirees	Total
1.	Pension	46	43	89 (44.5%)
2.	Pension+ Business	20	27	47 (23.5%)
3.	Pension+ Agriculture	11	12	33 (16.5%)
4.	Pension+Business+ Agriculture	10	6	16 (8%)
5.	Pension+ Post retirement job	13	12	25 (12.5%)
	Total	100	100	200 (100%)

Mr. K.L.N. Raju, a retired gazetted officer from Income–tax service, says; "I draw finances from a couple of sources. In addition to my pension which is nearly a thousand rupees, I get a house rent of Rs. 850 per month and yearly returns of about ten to fifteen thousands on 6 acres of dry land." So, income from these supplementary sources is greater than his pension and make his budget surplus.

Annual income

Table–21 shows the percentage distribution of the aged respondents by their levels of annual income from different sources. Almost two-thirds of the 200 sample retirees have an income between Rs. 3,001 and Rs. 12,000.

Among the gazetted retirees, there is none whose annual income is less than Rs. 3,000 because no gazetted retiree draws a monthly income of Rs. 250 or less. Almost three-fourths of them have income ranging from Rs. 7,001 to Rs.25,000 per annum while only one–fourth of them have an yearly income ranging from Rs. 3,001 and Rs. 7,000. On the other hand, almost one-quarter of the non-gazetted retirees have a yearly income of Rs. 3,000 and less. Nearly another quarter of them have an annual income varying from Rs. 7,001 to Rs. 12,000. Less than half have an annual income between Rs. 3,001 to Rs. 7,000 and only one-tenth of them have an annual income ranging from Rs. 12,000 to Rs. 25,000.

Table 21. Percentage Distribution of the Respondents according to their Annual Income

S.No.	Annual income in Rupees	Number of Gazetted Retirees	Number of Non-gazetted Retirees	Total
1.	Upto 3000	—	23	23 (11.5%)
2.	3001 to 7000	24	44	68 (34%)
3.	7001 to 12000	41	23	64 (32%)
4.	12001 to 25000	35	10	45 (22.5%)
	Total	100	100	200 (100%)

't' value= 0.9212 (not significant)

The difference in income patterns of the respondents reveals the differential financial positions between gazetted and non-gazetted retirees. But the income of considerable proportion of the non-gazetted retirees is on par with that of the gazetted retirees. This can be attributed to a vast majority of the former's income from other sources like agricultural and house rents. The above finding supports the hypothesis which states:

Retirees in the more highly paid occupations have more savings and other resources for retirement than do the retirees in the jobs drawing lower pay.

Expenditure

Table-22 gives the percentage distribution of the aged respondents according to their annual expenditure. The maximum number of the gazetted respondents incur an annual expenditure between Rs. 3,001 and Rs. 12,000. On the other hand, the maximum number of non-gazetted respondents incur an annual expenditure ranging from less than Rs. 3,000 to Rs. 7,000.

A comparison of Table-24 and 25 shows that out of the 35 percent gazetted retirees who have an annual income of more than Rs. 12,000 only 15 percent are spending the whole income. Similarly out of the 10 percent of the non-gazetted retirees with an annual income above Rs. 12,000, only 3 percent are spending the total income. All this reflects the ingrained savings habit in the aged people.

Table 22. Percentage Distribution of the Retirees according to their Annual Expenditure

S.No.	Annual Expenditure	Number of Gazetted Retirees	Number of Non-gazetted Retirees	Total
1.	Upto 3000	8	33	44 (20.5%)
2.	3001 to 7000	42	54	96 (48%)
3.	7001 to 12000	35	10	45 (22.5%)
4.	12001 to 25000	15	3	18 (9%)
	Total	100	100	200 (100%)

't' value = 5.7648 (significant at 0.01 level)

Table 23. Percentage Distribution of the Retirees according to the Method of Distribution of their properties

S.No.	Method of distribution of property	Number of Gazetted Retirees	Number of Non-gazetted Retirees	Total
1.	Wish to keep with oneself till alive	33	35	68 (34%)
2.	Execute a will	14	7	21 (10.5%)
3.	Give a share to wife	20	11	31 (15.5%)
4.	Distribute amongst children during life-time	15	11	26 (13%)
5.	Give the children who who serve in old age	18	36	54 (27%)
	Total	100	100	200 (100%)

Discretion of the aged regarding their propertie

Table-23 gives the percentage distribution of the respondents according to the method of distribution of their properties. Slightly more than one-third have answered that they wish to keep their properties with themselves till alive. There is not much difference in number between the gazetted and non-gazetted retirees who gave the above answers.

When asked about their idea regarding the distribution of their property, 34 percent of the total retirees in the ratio of 1:1 told that they wish to keep the property with themselves so long as they are alive, to be distributed only to their legal heirs after their demise. Gazetted verses non-gazetted retirees in the ratio of 2:1 have executed their will and testament regarding the distribution of their property.

The figures indicate a sense of more insecurity among the non-gazetted retirees than in the gazetted retirees. The same conclusion is also possible from the fact that 18 percent of the gazetted retirees and twice this number of the non-gazetted retirees answered that they will give the property to those children who serve them in the old-age.

M.S.R.K. Prasad, a retired teacher, says; "I have distributed my little property among my two sons and my daughter who are now frequently visiting me and properly taking care after me and my wife." The above observation is significant in that it speaks about healthier care from children's side even after distribution of property during the retiree's life-time.

ANNUAL BUDGETS

Budget heads

In order to present a comprehensive budgetary position of the respondents, the following case studies are made out of the 200 retirees. Social and religious ceremonies play a dominant role in the lives of all employees and their families. They give more importance to social ceremonies and spend more money on them. During the festival time they spend heavily. The average expenditure on social ceremonies such as puberty, marriage, child-birth, naming and tonsuring and death will be about Rs. 200, Rs. 5,000, Rs. 800, Rs. 200 and Rs. 2,000 respectively.

Table 24. Details of Income and Expenditure of the Family of Mr. Adinarayana during 1987-88

Source of Income	Amount of income in Rupees	Items of expenditure	Amount in Rupees
Pension	5,850	Food	6,262
Agriculture	4,720	Clothing	1,000
		House repair	500
		Medical charges	200
		House tax	450
		Electricity bill	350
		Tailoring charges	250
		Newspaper charges	450
		Festivals	640
		Agricultural expenses	1,330
Total	10,570	Total	12,032

Deficit budget

Mr. Adinarayana is a retired non-gazetted employee. He worked as a Lower Division Clerk in a Government office. His family includes himself, his wife and three children. During 1987-88, he got an annual income of Rs. 10,570 by way of retirement benefits. He has three acres of dry land in which his tenant grows groundnut. He gets about 23 bags of groundnut per crop from his land. Thus his annual income from his land for the two crops of groundnut raised in it is Rs. 4,720. The following table discloses the annual income and expenditure of his family. It reveals a deficit budget to the tune of Rs. 1,462.

Mr. K. Sadasiva Murthy, aged 63, is a retired gazetted officer from Andhra Pradesh Government. He worked in the Department of Agriculture as an agricultural officer. In the year 1987-88 he got a pension of around Rs. 2,083 per mensum with which he runs a deficit budget. He has two daughters and a son of whom only the eldest daughter is married and settled in life. The other two are still college going children. This respondent is not left with any property. The annual income of the respondent comes to nearly Rs. 25,000. The deficit Rs. 2,600 is met by raising hand loans.

Surplus budget

Mr. Rama Mohana Rao, aged 64, worked as a Superintendent in the Public Works Department at Anantapur. He was a non-gazetted

Table 25. Details of Income and Expenditure of the Family of Mr. Sadasiva Murthy in the year 1987-88

Source of Income	Amount in Rupees	Items of expenditure	Amount in Rupees
Pension	25,000	House rent	7,200
		Food	15,000
		Clothing	3,000
		Medical charges	500
		Newspaper	450
		Festivals	250
		Education	1,200
Total	25,000	Total	27,600

Table 26. Details of Income and Expenditure of the Family of Mr. Rama Mohana Rao in the year 1987-88

Source of Income	Amount in Rupees	Items of expenditure	Amount in Rupees
Pension	8,500	Food	9,663
Agriculture	6,900	Fuel charges (gas, kerosene)	1,000
House rents	1,160		
		Clothing	240
		Medical Charges	250
		House tax	330
		Electricity bill	350
		House repairs	200
		News paper	500
		Agricultural Expenses	2,323
Total	16,560	Total	14,726

officer. He gets an annual income of Rs. 16,560 of which Rs. 8,500 is from his pension and the remaining Rs. 8,060 is from his farm and house rents. He has four children who are married and presently he is living with his wife and one of his married sons. He owns quite a big house in the town. Part of it, a small room with attached bath room and toilet, is let out from which he gets a rental of Rs. 1,160. From agriculture he receives a pension of Rs. 8,500. His total annual income is thus Rs. 16,560 and he runs a surplus budget as shown in the following table.

The above table reveals that Mr. Rama Mohana Rao runs a surplus budget by saving Rs. 2,260 every year.

Mr. Krishnaiah Chetty is a retired gazetted officer from Andhra Pradesh Government service. He gets an annual income around Rs. 31,230 of which Rs. 24,370 is from his salary and the remaining Rs. 6,850 is from interests on deposits. His three children are now studying in local colleges; the eldest is studying engineering, the second one his graduate course in sciences; and the last one his intermediate. His family incurs an expenditure of Rs. 26,986 every year. So he runs a surplus budget.

Table 27. The Income and Expenditure of the Family of Mr. Krishnaiah Chetty with surplus Budget during the year 1987-88

Source of Income	Amount in Rupees	Items of expenditure	Amount in Rupees
Pension	24,370	Food	24,200
Interest on deposits	6,860	Clothing	672
		Education	523
		Medical Bill	224
		Recreation	276
		Electricity Bill	246
		Fuel / Gas Bill	550
		Others	295
Total	31,230	Total	26,986

Table–27 shows the income and expenditure of his family in the year 1987-88.

Balanced budget

Mr. Narasimhachari, aged 68 years, retired as an Elementary School Teacher. His family includes seven members: himself, his wife, his two married sons, his two daughters-in-law and his grand child. One of his sons, aged 32 years, is temporarily employed as a Clerk in the Tirumala-Tirupati Temple Administrative Office. Another son, aged 29 years, is working as a teacher in the local High School. He receives an annual pension of Rs. 7,330. His son working as a teacher gets an annual income of Rs. 14,733 and his other son working as a Clerk gets an annual income of Rs. 12,767. The annual income of the family thus comes to Rs. 37,380. However, since Mr. Narasimhachari has to maintain a large family, a major part of the income is to be spent on food and clothing. The following table shows the income and expenditure of Mr. Narasimhachari 's family.

The table reveals that the family budget of Mr. Narasimhachari includes neither deficit nor surplus. Thus this family can be taken as an example of a balanced budget among the retired employees.

Mr. Raja Reddy is a retired engineer from the Andhra Pradesh State Electricity Board. His yearly income from salary is Rs. 16,870.

Table 28. Details of Income and Expenditure of the Family of Mr. Narasimhachari during the Year 1987-88

Source of Income	Amount in Rupees	Items of expenditure	Amount in Rupees
Pension of Father	7,330	Food	20,334
		Clothing	5,312
Salary of the eldest son	14,733	Marriage and festivals	1,365
Slary of the younger son	12,767	House-tax	400
		Electricity	400
		Transport charges	200
		Newspaper charges	450
		Medical charges	291
		Smoking	1,260
		Drinking	2,310
		Travel	660
		Others	2,940
Total	35,830	Total	35,830

His son is married. He is working as a lower division clerk. His annual salary comes to Rs. 15,769. He owns three acres of farm land in his native village. He leased it to his brother who raises two crops a year. He gets paddy worth of Rs. 2,534 every year from the two rice crops grown in that field. There are five members in his family: himself, his wife, his married son, his daughter-in-law, and his grandson. His family's total income in the year 1987-88 was Rs. 35,063. He spent all the income for his family. This shows his balanced budget.

Adequacy of Income

Table-30 reveals the percentage distribution of the retirees according to the adequacy of their income in the year 1987-88. It is very apparent from the table that those having adequate income among the gazetted are more than twice the number of non-gazetted among the retirees.

The above table shows that the income of the gazetted retirees is more than that of the non-gazetted retirees. The gazetted with higher official status and more income than the non-gazetted, have

Table 29. The Income and Expenditure of Mr. Raja Reddy's Family with Balanced Budget during the Year 1987-88

Source of Income	Amount in Rupees	Items of expenditure	Amount in Rupees
Pension of father	16,870	Food	24,875
Salary of son	15,769	Clothing	3,562
Agriculture	2,534	Smoking	454
		Drinking	1,605
		Socio-religious Functions	1,553
		Medical expenses	256
		Cinema	608
		Travel	2,150
Total	35,063	Total	35,063

adequate income. However, as income from other sources also support the retirees, a considerable number of the non-gazetted retirees felt their income is adequate, but again this is not the case with all the retirees. As a result, around one-fourth of the gazetted and more than half of the non-gazetted have answered on the negative about their income adequacy.

Table 30. Percentage Distribution of the Retirees according to the Adequacy of their Income in the year 1987-88

S.No.	Adequacy of income	Number of Gazetted Retirees	Number Non-gazetted Retirees	Total
1.	Adequate	73	38	111(55.5%)
2.	Inadequate	27	62	89 (44.5%)
	Total	100	100	200 (100%)

Chi Square value = 24.8001 (Significant at 1% level)

Mr. M. Hanumappa, aged 67, a non-gazetted retiree from Panchayatraj Department, has his wife, son and daughter. He says, "My income is adequate to meet my routine requirement. As I could save a little during my career, it is added to my pension. My savings and my pension are supporting me. So I need not depend on my children financially."

Mr. K. Shanta Prasad, aged 62, who lives with his wife, son and two daughters, says; "Even after retiring as a Gazetted Officer and drawing a moderate pension and having some savings, I am not able to meet with the routine expenditure. The reason is the inefficiency of my son in managing the financial matters of the family."

The above two case studies are recorded because with less income Hanumappa is feeling adequate and with more income Shanta Prasad is feeling inadequate due to various factors.

FINANCIAL MANAGEMENT

Financial help received during crises

Table-31 shows the percentage distribution of the retirees according to help received by them from different sources in their financial crises. Nearly half the number of 200 retirees receive financial help from their male children. In this context, more non-gazetted than gazetted officers received monetary help from their sons, after retirement.

Table 31. Percentage Distribution of the Retirees according to the Help received in Financal Crises

S.No.	Help received from	Number of Gazetted Retirees	Number Non-gazetted Retirees	Total
1.	Sons	43	52	95 (47.5)
2.	Daughters	17	8	25 (12.5%)
3.	Other relatives	10	5	15 (7.5%)
4.	Friends	30	35	65 (32.5 %)
	Total	100	100	200 (100%)

Chi square value =6.1439 (Not significant)

Table–31 also reveals that the friends of the retirees constituted the second highest group who have assisted the retirees financially while daughters and other relatives lagged behind. This pattern is the same in the gazetted as well as the non- gazetted retirees. Obviously the aged people have felt it their right to seek assistance and the sons felt their duty to comply with the demand. It is a custom in Indian families that the daughters are always given things from their parents but are not expected to give things to their parents.

Social functions and ceremonies affecting financial positions

Table-32 gives the percentage distribution of the aged according to their perception of social functions and ceremonies affecting their financial positions. It is quite apparent and vivid from the table that more than half of the total respondents have been affected financially by social functions and ceremonies which important phenomena in the financial life of the aged.

The income of the non-gazetted retirees is less than that of the non-gazetted retirees. Hence, money spent on marriages, house-warming celebrations and similar important occasions affect more the financial position of the non-gazetted retirees than the gazetted retirees. The ratio of the people affected and not affected among the non-gazetted category is approximately 3:1 while the same ratio among the gazetted employees is approximately 1:1.5. the presence of a few non-gazetted employees in not affected lot is due to their

Table 32. Percentage Distribution of the Retirees according to their Perceptions on Social Functions and Ceremonies affecting their Financial Positions

S.No.	Response	Number of Gazetted Retirees	Number of Non-gazetted Retirees	Total
1.	Affect	38	73	111 (55.5%)
2.	Don't affect	62	27	89 (44.5%)
	Total	100	100	200 (200%)

Chi Square Value = 24.8001 (Significant at 1% level)

income from other sources like house rents, agriculture and business, in addition to their pension.

Mr. P. Pandu Ranga Rao, aged 65, a retired teacher, says; "Social functions and ceremonies have no bearing upon my financial position." He could not give concrete reasons justifying the above statement. But observations reveal that, at times they affect and at times they don't, that is, there is a balance between these two and hence the neutrality.

Management of finances

Table–33 reveals the percentage distribution of the retirees according to their financial control and management. In the case of almost 50 percent of the retirees from both the gazetted and non-gazetted categories, the retirees along with their wives, manage their family finances.

It is of interest to note from the table that more than three-fourths of the retirees from the gazetted and non-gazetted categories have agreed that they run their financial affairs alone and manage the house or jointly control their financial position along with their wives. Relinquishing of the financial control to the wife occurred only in one-eighth of the total retirees. In this aspect there is not much of a significant different difference between the gazetted and the non-gazetted groups. A majority of the retirees managing the

Table 33. Percentage Distribution of the Retirees according to the Management of their Finance

S.No.	Response	Number of Gazetted Retirees	Number Non-gazetted Retirees	Total
1.	Self	40	30	70 (35%)
2.	Self & wife jointly	45	50	95 (47.5%)
3.	Wife	—	—	
4.	Self and others	10	15	25 (12.5%)
5.	Others	5	5	10 (5%)
	Total	100	100	200 (100%)

Chi Square Value = 2.6917 (Not significant)

financial affairs either themselves or with their wives jointly may be attributed to the fact that the retirees are afraid of their sons deserting them if the control is transferred to the latter, the moving factor is the association of 'gerontocracy' among the aged, that is, the flair for power among the retirees may also make them hold control and management over the family members. Right from childhood the general tendency of a son towards his mother is taking lenience and getting money or any other similar want. After attaining adulthood this tendency may change into authority where the son may override the mother and take away money or whatever he wants. So this is also one factor considered by the retirees for keeping control over property with self and wife jointly. Where the male retiree is physically incapable for running financial matters, his wife is given the authority to take control over the situation because the retiree felt that children have not come of age to shoulder such responsibilities.

Cause for living with children after retirement

Table-34 gives the percentage distribution of the retirees according to the information as to why they live with their children.

The gazetted versus non-gazetted retirees in the ratio of 2 : 1 say that they are living with the children not only for economic support

Table 34. Percentage Distribution of the Retirees according to the Information as to why they Live with their Children

S.No.	Information	Number of Gazetted Retirees	Number of Non-gazetted Retirees	Total
1.	Because they give not only economic support but also company	50	25	75
2.	Because of economic support and emotional attachment	28	39	67
	Total	78	64	142

Chi Square Value = 10.1393 (Significant at 1% level)

but for having their company also. More non-gazetted retirees than gazetted retirees say that they have emotional attachment to children in addition to obtaining economic support which made them stay with their children. Whatever may be the reason given, it is felt that the retirees being old feel the need of their children and which is not only for their financial support but also for physical and emotional support.

PATTERNS OF ECONOMIC ADJUSTMENT

Bases and patterns of economic adjustment

After retirement choices are narrowed down in terms of income, one has to trim his economic needs according to the available finances. The way the retirees regulate their needs to suit their financial resources is, therefore, an important aspect of their total adjustment in old age. The modes of economic adjustment as practiced by the retirees, show some interesting facts.

On the basis of the income and the economic problems of the retirees besides the social pressures on them to make economic adjustments in the post-retirement situation, an attempt is made here to extract the different patterns of economic adjustment of the retirees. Accordingly, we will have three broad classes of retirees according to the respondent's own judgement of the standard of adequacy:

i. those with adequate post-retirement income

ii. those with inadequate post-retirement income; and

iii. those with marginal income

Retirees who think they have adequate income to overcome retirement problems may be considered well adjusted and people who feel inadequacy of income are mal-adjusted or poorly adjusted.

Generally retirees, as a way out of the economic problems, reduce their wants and needs according to their post-retirement income. Cutting short their needs affects the standard of living and also imposes sanctions on the social participation of the retirees.

Dependence on the savings is another solution to meet the post-retirement financial crisis. The savings and interest on the same would survive the retirees only to a limited period. As of now a large number of employees belong to the low-paid sections with meager salaries. A variety of sources and different persons would

Table 35. Percentage Distribution of the Retirees according to their Adjustment Patterns

S.No.	Adjustment pattern	Number of Gazetted Retirees	Number of Non-gazetted Retirees	Total
1.	The well adjusted	61	19	80 (40%)
2.	The poorly adjusted	22	55	77 (38.5%)
3.	The marginally adjusted	17	26	43 (21.5%)
	Total	100	100	200 (100%)

have been giving support while the retirees were in service. But those options are limited and the retiree is left with very limited finances now.

Along with these economic problems, there are psycho-social problems experienced by the retirees such as loneliness and isolation. Those who spend time without any post-retirement job suffer these more than those who engage themselves in some activity.

Table 35 reveals the percentage distribution of the retirees by their patterns of adjustment. Among the gazetted bulk are well adjusted but among the non-gazetted bulk are poorly adjusted. The marginally adjusted are the lowest in number among the gazetted but the well adjusted are the lowest in number among the non-gazetted.

The well-adjusted

The economic life of this group of retirees is very less disturbed. They are the old people who do not experience much hardships in Post-retirement on account of sudden fall in income from regular employment because they make good the deficiency by supplementing their income through various other sources. They somehow pull on the same standard of living and shield their status from running into problems that generally follow retirement. Relatively this group is experiencing a peaceful situation as economic responsibilities are not causing them any worry. For them, retirement is not an important economic event in their life as its adverse effects are concerned.

Also people who retire from high public positions like members of the Indian Administrative Service, persons holding senior positions in civil administration and other branches of the Government, persons who have inherited ancestral property or made their own property through personal efforts, and few others whose children are highly placed in India or abroad and provide all amenities of life to their old parents are better able to take care of their personal needs and social obligations. The following two cases are cited in support of this observation.

Mr. M. Seetharama Murthy is a sixty two year old man retired from the Secretariat of Tamil Nadu Government from a senior position. He has a good ancestral property. Before he retired, he constructed two big houses which yield a rent of Rs. 1800 per month. So this income adds to his pension which is really a good income to make a comfortable living.

The respondent has a son and a daughter. His son is a doctor and does not depend upon his father for economic needs. Daughter is a college student. He is maintaining a personal car, a telephone, and he has not curtailed his expenditure on food, drinks and other personal preferences.

So it is clear that a retiree placed in a good position before retirement, would not be much affected by his retirement so far as economic adjustment is concerned. The second case of well-adjusted retiree is cited below.

H.L. Narasimham retired from a top management rank. Two of his sons got higher education abroad and settled there comfortably. The respondent and his wife have also been abroad at the invitation of their sons. They have given their parents all the comforts.

The respondent has purchased a big residential building after his retirement. He has rented out some portions of the building and is getting regular income from his investment. He is also maintaining a personal telephone at his residence so that his sons may call him from abroad any time they like.

The poorly adjusted

Retirees who have reduced their economic needs as a result of reduced income would cut short their wants, consume their savings, take up jobs to supplement their meagre pensions or depend on the assistance from sons or other relatives. The immediate consequences of retirement are more prominent in their case. They are susceptive to experience anxiety, loss of social status and personal pride and tend to count time when they would have their economic problems completely solved. They have children who do not yet settle in self-sufficient positions or left unmarried and grand-children to be looked after due to the death of a son or son-in-law or otherwise, forced to keep up their position in the caste and kin group to ensure a good match for their daughters.

The poorly adjusted retirees are of a typical middle class type. They don't compromise with the present position and are ridden with emotions to satisfy the needs of their dependents, but in vain. Thus, the poorly-adjusted retirees are achieving financial adjustment at considerable personal cost in terms of protecting their social status and personality balance. The following case of retired gazetted officers brings out the point more clearly.

P. Sarathi was a gazetted officer in State Civil Service. During his service he was comfortable with the income. He was able to maintain a reasonably good position during his service career.

Presently, he is facing financial troubles. He suffered a huge loss on account of theft committed in his house after retirement. He has to dispose many articles to compensate the loss. The respondent has two sons and a daughter, all of whom are married. His family consists of his wife and a married son with his wife and a child. This is a joint household. The respondent does not get any financial help from his sons. His second son lives in Visakhapatnam where he works in the Harbour as an engineer, the son who is living with the respondent is supported by his father partially. He feels that his sons should shoulder their own responsibilities but the traditional prestige of the family is standing in his way to deal with his sons.

The respondent is highly status conscious. He said; "I have a high status while in service and the people around me expect a certain level of life from me." He is not able to maintain the relations with his friends and relatives owing to loss of status. He finds it equally difficult to mix up with the lower grade people. His financial troubles are deepening due to events like death, birth, marriage and others.

The marginally adjusted

This group consists of retirees who are facing financial problem but again balancing them with the available resources. There are totally 43 retirees who come under this category. Naturally more number of non-gazatted retirees are found in this category for is a style of life even before their retirement was of financial marginality. Some of them are not only economically handicapped but their family and social life are equally troubled owing to financial reasons.

Mr. M. Babu Rao, a retired non-gazetted employees, says; "My experiences are such that they taught me living barely with minimal needs." He retired as a school teacher and is re-employed in a private school as a teacher on a meagre salary. His parents expired when he was a child and was brought up by his father's brother.

Mr. R. Krishna Prasad is a retired gazetted officer from University service. His wife suffers from cancer. He said with a sense of grief that he could not enjoy his life any time. He has three children who are grown up and settled in their life. Straining every nerve he brought up all his children and made them settle in their life. This is what he could achieve in his career. So he says he could not cross a certain economic point in his total life.

The economic situation of the aged is understood by seeing the different patterns and different cases. For many economic hardships are natural results of their low income and poor economic status. Large families and dependent children are the other major reasons which can be attributed to the marginally and poorly adjusted categories.

Contrary to the western style of life, in India parents are expected to not only bring up their children but also to settle them till they get married. This is a common scene in most of the Indian families. Even though adult sons are expected to support their old parents, it is rarely seen that the aged parents are receiving the full support of their children.

Family Adjustment 7

This chapter discusses the structural and organization adjustment of the family of the gazetted and non-gazetted retirees. In this connection, it shows the changes that have taken place with reference to the types of family and tries to answer several questions. What were the types of family? What were the types of the family at the time for retirement? What decisions the retirees had taken to bring the types of the family existing at the time of retirement into what they are now after retirement? How much time the retirees had taken to adjust their family at the time of retirement to the present type of the family? Who exactly were the persons involved in this total process?

While dealing with the present organization aspect, this chapter describes the management and the decision-making activities, the dependence of the aged on children, and certain changes in interpersonal relations within the present framework of the family. The description highlights the different forms of management that the retirees adopted to have a hold on the family property, and the distinct types of decision-making over the family matters to have some hold on the children despite identification of generation gap in social, economic, political and other realms.

PRESENT FAMILY

Size of the family

Table 36 shows the percentage distribution of the families of the two hundred retirees according to their size. More than one-fourth of the total number of families of the retirees comprise two-member ones.

Among the gazetted and the non-gazetted retirees the two-member and the four-member families are numerically dominant over the other families. Among the one-member families those of the gazetted are more than twice that of the non-gazetted. This is a reflection of more number of spinsters among the gazetted retirees who are leading a long life. But the two-member families among the non-gazetted are one and half times more than those among the gazetted retirees. Whereas a vast majority of the two-member families are the residues left after the children moved to other places on account of either employment or marriage, the remaining number of the two-member families are a result of childlessness of the couples and economic maladjustment between the aged retirees and their employed children and the consequent separate living of the retirees and their children.

The three-member and the four-member families together comprise almost forty percent of the total number of the families. Three and four member families come under the ideal family size as perceived by the respondents. So, the numerical dominance of these families reflects the views of the respondents on ideal family size.

The five-member families among the gazetted are slightly more in number than those among the non-gazetted. Impact of family planning methods was not significant on these respondents, even though its importance is well known to the respondents.

Table 36. Percentage Distribution of the Facilities of the Retirees according to their Sizes

S. No.	Size of the Family	Number of the families		Total
		Gazetted	Non-Gazetted	
1.	One member	5	2	7 (3.5%)
2.	Two members	18	29	47 (23.5%)
3.	Three members	17	12	29 (14.5%)
4.	Four members	26	24	50 (25.0%)
5.	Five members	19	16	35 (17.5%)
6.	Six members	11	9	20 (10%)
7.	Seven members	4	8	12 (6%)
	Total	100	100	200 (100%)

The six-member families comprise one-tenth of the total sample, and the seven-member are even less than the six-member ones. Retirees in this category are older in whose time large families were quite common.

So it is clear from the table that as slightly more than sixty percent of he retirees are aware of the consequences and problems of large families, they are maintaining small families.

Genealogical Composition

Table-37 shows the percentage distribution of the present families of the retirees according to their genealogical composition. The age of the retirees is in correspondence with the genealogical complexity of the family. No family among both the categories of the retirees embraces four generations for none of the retirees attained the age of 80 years or more to see his great-grand children.

Among the retirees while the families including members of two generations comprise almost 50 percent of the total number of the families, the one-generation and the three-generation families comprise the other 50 percent of the total member of the families.

The one-generation families among the gazetted and non-gazetted are almost equal in their proportions. A small proportion of these families include childless couples but a vast majority of these families include aged couples who formed as residues after the separation of their children from them.

The two-generation families among the gazetted retirees are one and half times of those among the non-gazetted retirees. This is

Table 37. Percentage Distribution of the present Families of the Retirees according to their Genealogical Composition

S.No.	Number of generation	Number of Gazetted Retirees	Number Non-gazetted Retirees	Total
1.	One	25	29	54 (27%)
2.	Two	56	38	94 (47%)
3.	Three	19	29	48 (24%)
	Total	100	100	200 (100%)

because the gazetted employees, unlike the non-gazetted ones, perform late marriages for their children.

The three-generation families among the non-gazetted retirees are more than one and half times of those among the gazetted retirees. The reason is that more number of the non-gazetted retirees prefer to live with their married children for security purpose. When the retirees live with their married children it is but natural that the grand-children come into picture.

Type of the family

Table-38 reveals the percentage distribution of the families of the respondents according to their type. A little less than half the number of retirees are living with their spouses and unmarried children. In this context, it is found that a vast majority among the gazetted and only a little more than one-third among the non-gazetted live with their spouses and children. This shows the stronger intention of the gazetted than that of the non-gazetted to live with their grown-up children after retirement.

The table shows the numerical predominance of nuclear families over the other types of families among both the gazetted and non-gazetted retirees. Nuclear and extended families comprise a little less than three-fourths and nearly one-fourth respectively of the total number of families. Single member households occur among the gazetted as well as the non-gazetted retirees to the extent of nearly four percent.

There are 7 retirees who are living alone. Of these, 5 are gazetted and 2 are non-gazetted retirees. They have not lived alone under three distinct types of situations.

i. 3 of them, 2 among the gazetted retirees and one among the non-gazetted members, are spinsters. They got accustomed to independent life throughout their career, hence even after retirement they did not wish to stay with any of their relatives.

ii. 3 of them, two among the gazetted retirees and one among the non-gazetted retirees, have formed when their male or female spouses pre-deceased them and they preferred to live away from their married children due to family feuds and misunderstandings.

iii. One of them, found only among the gazetted retirees, is a

Table 38. Percentage Distribution of the Families of the Retirees according to their Structural Types

S.No.	Type of the family	Number of Gazetted Retirees	Number of Non-gazetted Retirees	Total
1.	Living alone			
	i. Spinsters	2	1	3 (1.50%)
	ii. Widowers	1	1	2 (1.00%)
	iii. Widow	1	—	1 (0.50%)
	iv. Husband living away from wife and children	1	—	1 (0.50%)
	Sub-Total	5	2	7 (3.05%)
2.	Nuclear family			
	i. Incomplete nuclear family	26	24	50 (25.00%)
	ii. Incomplete nuclear family with dependents	5	7	12 (6.00%)
	iii. Complete nuclear families	31	31	62 (31.00%)
	iv. Complete nuclear family with dependents	10	12	22 (11.00%)
	Sub-Total	72	74	146 (73.00%)
3.	Extended family			
	i. Complete vertically extended family	13	12	25 (12.50%)
	ii. Complete horizontally extended family with dependents	4	3	7. (3.50%)
	iii. Complete horizontally extended family	6	9	15 (7.50%)
	Sub-Total	23	24	47 (23.50%)
	Total	100	100	200 (100%)

Chi-square value = 6.6336 (Significant at 5% level)
Note : Types of family explained in Appendix II

male who shunned family life. He is living alone of his own volition forsaking family contacts with his wife and with his grown up sons. His wife is living with one of his sons. A few years before his retirement this officer lost interest in worldly affairs and resigned to family life.

Of the 146 nuclear families, 72 belong to the gazetted and 74 to the non-gazetted retirees. Among the nuclear families the complete nuclear families form almost one-thirds of the total number of families. There are 50 incomplete nuclear families whose composition presents a single pattern formed under two different sets of circumstances.

i. 5 of these, 2 belonging to the gazetted retirees and 3 belonging to the non-gazetted retirees, include childless couples.

ii. 45 of these, of whom 24 belong to the gazetted retirees and 21 belong to the non-gazetted retirees, have formed when the couples lost their only child, lost their dependents, remained as residues after the married children established their separate families. Also employment of children elsewhere led to the conditions of incompleteness among some respondents.

There are 12 incomplete nuclear families with dependents, 5 among the gazetted and 7 among the non-gazetted retirees. They acquired their composition under three types of situations.

i. 2 families, one each among the gazetted and non-gazetted retirees, have a composition that includes a man, his wife, and his dependent namely the unmarried sister of his wife.

ii. 4 families, 2 each among the gazetted and non-gazetted retirees, have a composition that includes a man, his wife and his wife's sister's daughter who is studying in a college.

iii. 4 families, one among the gazetted and three among the non-gazetted retirees, have a structure that consists of a man, his wife and a distant relative who is a dependent.

iv. One family among the gazetted retirees consists of a man, his wife and his father's sister who is a dependent.

v. One family among the non-gazetted retirees includes a man, his wife and his wife's elder brother who is a dependent.

There are 62 complete nuclear families each of which includes a couple and their unmarried children. They have formed under four distinct situations.

i. 41 of these,22 among the gazetted and 19 among the non-gazetted retirees, have a single pattern of composition which includes a man, his wife , his unmarried daughters and sons. His married children are living in several places.

ii. 16 of these, 8 each among the gazetted and non-gazetted retirees, have a composition that includes a man, his wife and his unmarried son or sons. Some of them have married daughter or daughters who are living in their husbands' families.

iii. 4 of these, one among the gazetted and 3 among the non-gazetted retirees, have a composition which includes a couple and their unmarried daughters. None of their daughters are married although they have come of age.

iv. One family among the gazetted retirees includes a man, his daughter borne by his first wife who pre-deceased him, and his two daughters borne by his second wife whom he married after the demise of his first wife.

There are 22 complete nuclear families with dependents, 10 among the gazetted and 12 among the non-gazetted retirees. They acquired their composition under eight types of situations.

i. 8 families 5 among the gazetted and 3 among the non-gazetted retirees, have a composition that includes a man, his wife , and his sons besides his widowed father or mother as a dependent.

ii. 4 families, 1 among the gazetted and 3 among the non-gazetted retirees, acquired a structure whereby each consists of a man, his wife, his children and his widowed father-in-law or mother-in-law as a dependent.

iii. One gazetted retiree's family includes himself, his wife, his son and his daughter and his elder brother who is physically handicapped hence a dependent.

iv. 2 families, one each among the gazetted and non-gazetted retirees, have a composition that shows a man, his wife, his children and his widowed elder sister who is a dependent.

v. 2 families, one each among the gazetted and non-gazetted retirees, have acquired a structure that includes a man, his wife, his children and his wife's widowed elder sister who is a dependent.

vi. 2 families, one each among the gazetted and non-gazetted retirees, includes a man, his wife, his children and his distant relative, who is a dependent.

vii. One family among the non-gazetted retirees includes a man, his wife, his child and his father's sister who is sunk in senility.

viii. 2 families among the non-gazetted have a structure that includes a man and his children and his daughter's son as a temporary dependent

There are 47 extended families. Of these, 25 are complete vertically extended families, 7 are complete vertically extended families with dependent and 15 are horizontally extended families. The 25 complete vertically extended families show a single pattern of composition acquired under different circumstances.

i. 12 families, 6 among the gazetted and 6 among the non-gazetted retirees, have a composition which includes a man, his wife, his married son , his son's wife, and his son's child or children.

ii. 13 families, 7 among the gazetted retirees and 6 among the non-gazetted retirees, have a composition embracing a man, his wife, his married son, his son's wife and his son's children. His other son or sons who are married are living elsewhere with their independent families.

There are 7 complete vertically extended families with dependents of which 4 belong to the gazetted retirees and 3 belong to the non-gazetted retirees. They acquired similar composition with a difference only with reference to their dependents.

i. 4 families, 2 each among the gazetted and non-gazetted retirees have a composition that includes a man, his son, his son's wife, and his son's children and his widowed mother or father as a dependent.

ii. One among the gazetted includes a man, his wife, his son, his son's wife and his son's children and his dependent namely widowed sister who crossed her sixtieth year.

iii. 2 families, one each among the gazetted and non-gazetted retirees, have a composition that includes a man, his wife, his son's wife and his son's children and his daughters son or daughter who is a dependent till his or her education is completed.

There are 15 complete horizontally extended families which show almost a similar pattern of composition formed under two types of situations.

i. 13 families, 4 among the gazetted and 9 among the non-gazetted retirees, have a composition in which two or more married brothers, their spouses, and their children are living together. They own the property in common. They have a common hearth and they live in a single house.

ii. 2 families among the gazetted retirees have acquired a structure according to which brothers, their wives, and their children are living together. Each family has joint property by each brother with his wife and children lives in a separate house built in a single compound.

FAMILY AT THE TIME OF RETIREMENT

Proportions of different types of family

Table-39 shows the types of family of the respondents at the time of their retirement. Almost three-fourths of the total number of families belonged to different sub-types of nuclear family. A little less than one-fourth of the total number of the families were extended. Only 2 percent of the domestic units included persons who were living alone. The nuclear as well as the extended families occurred almost in equal proportions among the gazetted and non-gazetted respondents. However the respondents living alone were in 3:1 ratio among the gazetted and non-gazetted respondents at the time of their retirement.

Formation of different types of family

An analysis of the different types of family at the time of retirement of the respondents reveals different types of situations for the formation of these families. There were 4 respondents living alone under two distinct types of situations.

i. 3 respondents, 2 among the gazetted and 1 among the non-gazetted retirees, were living alone because they were

Table 39. Percentage Distribution of the Families of the Respondents according to their structural Types at the Time of Retirement

S.No.	Type of the family	Number of Gazetted Retirees	Number of Non-gazetted Retirees	Total
1.	Living alone			
	i. Spinsters	2	1	3 (1.50%)
	ii. Husband living away from wife and children	1	—	1 (0.50%)
	Sub-Total	3	1	4 (2.00%)
2.	Nuclear family			
	i. Incomplete nuclear family	20	17	37 (18.5%)
	ii. Incomplete nuclear family with dependents	8	9	17 (8.50%)
	iii. Complete nuclear families	27	32	59 (29.5%)
	iv. Complete nuclear family with dependents	19	17	36 (18.00%)
	Sub-Total	74	75	149 (74.50%)
3.	Extended family			
	i. Incomplete vertically extended family	2	1	3 (1.50%)
	ii. Complete vertically extended family	14	13	27 (13.5%)
	iii. Complete horizontally extended family with dependents	1	1	2 (1.00%)
	iv. Incomplete horizontally extended family	2	1	3 (1.50%)
	v. Complete horizontally extended family	3	6	9 (4.50%)
	vi. Complete horizontally extended family with dependents	1	2	3 (1.50%)
	Sub-Total	23	24	47 (23.50%)
	Total	100	100	200 (100%)

spinsters and preferred to have single blessedness forever.

ii. One respondent who was a non-gazetted employee refrained from worldly pleasures including family life.

Of the 149 nuclear families, 37 were incomplete nuclear, 17 were incomplete nuclear with dependents, 59 were complete nuclear, and 36 were complete nuclear with dependents. The 37 incomplete nuclear families formed under five sets of circumstances.

i. 5 of these respondents, 2 among the gazetted and 3 among the non-gazetted retirees, were childless couples throughout their life.

ii. 3 respondents, one among the gazetted and two among the non-gazetted, reported that their only child died and so they were left alone.

iii. 16 respondents, 10 among the gazetted and 6 among the non-gazetted, had daughters who were married and moved to their husband's families in accordance with the rule of patrilocality.

iv. 9 respondents, 5 among the gazeted and 4 among the non-gazetted, each had a son and daughter and the daughter after her marriage left for her husband's family and the son who was employed and married, established a family at the place of his employment. So, the old couple were left as a residue.

v. 4 respondents, 2 among the gazetted, lost their wives, hence a composition consisting of a man and his children. Some of the children who were married left their natal families while others are still young and unmarried.

The 17 incomplete nuclear families with dependents had acquired their composition under three sets of circumstances.

i. 4 families, 2 each among the gazetted and non-gazetted retirees, had a composition consisting of a man and his wife and his dependents namely his widower father, widowed mother, widowed sister or widowed father's brother.

ii. 9 families, 5 among the gazetted and 4 among the non-gazetted, had a composition embràcing a man and his wife and his dependent namely his widower father-in-law, widowed mother-in-law, widowed mother-in-law's sister, widowed mother-in-law's mother, wife's younger brother, wife's younger sister or daughter's father-in-law.

iii. 4 families, one among the gazetted and three among the non-gazetted, had a structure consisting of a man and his wife and his or her distant and aged male and female relatives as dependents.

The 59 complete nuclear families of the respondents before their retirement formed under four sets of circumstances.

i. 14 families, 6 among the gazetted and 8 among the non-gazetted, had a composition which embraced a man, his wife and his son or sons.

ii. 11 families, 5 among the gazetted and 6 among the non-gazetted, had each included a man, his wife and his daughter or daughters.

iii. 33 families, 15 among the gazetted and 18 among the non-gazetted, had each consisted of a man, his wife, his son or sons and his daughter or daughters.

iv. One family among the gazetted included a man, a daughter borne by his first wife who is no more and his second wife and two daughters borne by the second wife.

Among the complete nuclear families those which contained a couple and their unmarried male and female children were more common than those which included a couple and their male children or a couple and their female children, those which included two sets of children, one borne by the first wife and the other borne by the second wife, were very rare.

There were 36 complete nuclear families with dependents which came into existence under a variety of circumstances.

i. 4 families, 2 each among the gazetted and non-gazetted retirees, had a composition that included a man, his wife his sons and his dependent widower father.

ii. 5 families, 3 among the gazetted and 2 among the non-gazetted, each embraced a man, his wife, his sons and his widowed mother.

iii. 2 families, one among the gazetted and one among the non-gazetted, each contained a man, his wife, his sons and daughters and his dependent sister who had come of age.

iv. One family among the gazetted consisted of a man, his wife, his son and daughter and his dependent elder brother who was a physically disabled person.

v. 2 families, one each among the gazetted and the non-gazetted, had a composition that included a man, his wife and his two children besides his aged widowed sister who was a dependent.

vi. 2 families, one each among the gazetted and the non-gazetted, had a structure that included a man, his wife, his children and his dependent namely wife's widowed elder sister.

vii. One family among the non-gazetted contained a man, his wife, his unmarried daughters and his dependent, namely wife's elder brother who remained unmarried because his physical condition was not good.

viii. 4 families, one among the gazetted and 3 among the non-gazetted, included a man, his wife, his children and his dependent widower father-in-law.

ix. 3 families, 2 among the gazetted and one among the non-gazetted, included each a man, his wife, his child or children, and his widowed mother-in-law.

x. One among the gazetted included a man, his wife, his sons and his maternal grand mother.

xi. 2 families, one each among the gazetted and non-gazetted, had a composition that embraced a man, his wife, his child or children and his aged father's sister.

xii. One among the gazetted included a man, his wife, his sons and his elder sister's husband who had become a paralytic patient shortly after his elder sister's death and who had none to look after him.

xiii. 2 families among the non-gazetted included a man, his wife, his children besides his elder daughter'son who became a destitute after the death of his parents in a car accident.

xiv. 4 families, 3 among the gazetted and one among the non-gazetted, included each man his wife, his unmarried children and a child of his son or daughter, who is living elsewhere.

xv. One family among the gazetted and one family among the non-gazetted included a man, his wife, his two sons and a distant relative who was a dependent because she had no property and had none to look after her.

In a vast majority of the families, the dependents were relatives who were mostly from paternal, maternal or in-law's side. Distant relatives becoming as dependents of a family were rare. Son's or daughter's children were temporary dependents. Widowed or disabled siblings were dependents of their natal families only when their in-law's families could not maintain them or failed to oblige the social norms to maintain them.

There were 47 extended families of which the vertically extended type formed the numerically pre-ponderant ones. The incomplete vertically extended families, 3 in number, formed under two different conditions.

i. 2 families, one each among the gazetted and non-gazetted, formed when a couple with their son, and son's wife lived together. Their sons married many years ago but so far did not beget children.

ii. One family among the gazetted acquired its composition when the only grand child of a man died three years after its birth. This family included a man, his wife, his son and his son's wife.

There were 27 complete vertically extended families among the respondents before their retirement. These families acquired their structure under different conditions.

i. 13 families, 7 among the gazetted, and 6 among the non-gazetted, had a composition that included a man, his wife, his son, his son's wife and his son's child or children.

ii. 14 families, 7 among the gazetted and 7 among the non-gazetted, acquired a composition which embraced a man, his wife, one of his married sons, his son's wife and his son's children. The other married son or sons were living away maintaining their individual families at different places.

The 2 complete vertically extended families with dependents had acquired their composition under two different conditions.

i. one family among the gazetted officers included a man, his wife, his son, his son's wife and his son's children besides daughter's daughter who was staying as a dependent for prosecuting her higher education for the last seven years.

ii. Another family which was found among the non-gazetted officers included a man, his wife, his son, his son's wife and his son's children. His daughter's son, a school going child, was staying with him.

Apart from the vertically extended families, there were 15 horizontally extended families of which 3 were incomplete horizontally extended, 11 were complete horizontally extended and one was complete horizontally extended family with dependents. The 3 in-complete horizontally extended families came into existence in two different situations.

i. 2 families, one each among the gazetted and the non-gazetted respondents, had a composition that embraced a man, his wife, his brother and his brother's wife. Neither he nor his brother had any child so far.

ii. One family among the gazetted respondents included a man, his wife, one of his married brothers and his brother's wife. He had no children. His brother was married three years ago. His other two brothers were living separately.

There were 9 complete horizontally extended families among the respondents at the time of their retirement. They formed under three different sets of circumstances.

i. 6 families, 2 among the gazetted and 4 among the non-gazetted, had a composition that included a man, his wife, his children, his brother, his brother's wife and his brother's children.

ii. One family among the gazetted including a man, his children one of his married brothers, his brother's wife and his brother's children. His other married brothers were maintaining their individual families at different places where they were employed.

iii. 2 families among the non-gazetted each included a man, his wife, his brother's wife, his brother's children. Himself and his brothers were living in separate houses within a single compound. However, they cooked at one hearth, and owned property in common.

There were 3 complete horizontally extended families with dependents. They acquired their structure in two different situations.

i. One among the gazetted included a man, his wife, his children, his brother, his brother's wife, and his brother's children and his widowed and aged sister who was a dependent.

ii. Two among the non-gazetted included each a man, his wife, his children, his brother's children and his aged paternal grand parent who crossed his ninety years and was a dependent.

DYNAMICS OF THE FAMLY

Continuity of and change in the family

Table–40 and Diagrams-1, 2 and 3 show the distribution of the present types of family at the time of retirement. They reveal the continuity and change in the types of family by depicting how some families at the time of retirement continued to keep up their forms to the present day and how some families at the time of retirement changed to acquire new forms in the last several years after retirement. In other words, the quantitative details in the Table and the Diagrams divulge how the present types of families came to be what they are from what they were to be at the time of retirement of the subjects.

The figures in the Table and Diagrams show that the nuclear families hold a place of primacy over the other types even at the retirement of the respondents. Almost three-fourths of the respondents lived in nuclear families at the time of their retirement. However, it may be pointed out that higher proportion of respondents lived in incomplete and complete nuclear families with dependents before their retirement. Now a lesser proportion of the retirees live in such types of families because some of the dependents who were ripe in years passed away, some who were sisters, sisters-in-law, brothers-in-law and other near relatives who came of age either moved to their husbands' families after marriage or moved to their natal families and some who were physically disabilitated or who were not maintaining good health right from their childhood died.

At the time of retirement three spinsters and one married man were living alone. Pre - and post-retirement figures relating to the types of families thus show an increase in the number of single-member households among the retirees.

On the other hand, there was almost a ten percent decrease in the proportion of extended families among the respondents after their retirement. However, the vertically extended families are found to be more common than the horizontally extended families among the respondents either at the time of retirement or at present.

The respondents had taken certain decisions either to continue or to change their family composition so as to enable themselves to adopt to different socio-economic and other conditions they had to face in their post-retirement life. The decision-making involved availability of choices and human resources, individual management skills and abilities, time factors, emotional support, and social and economic security.

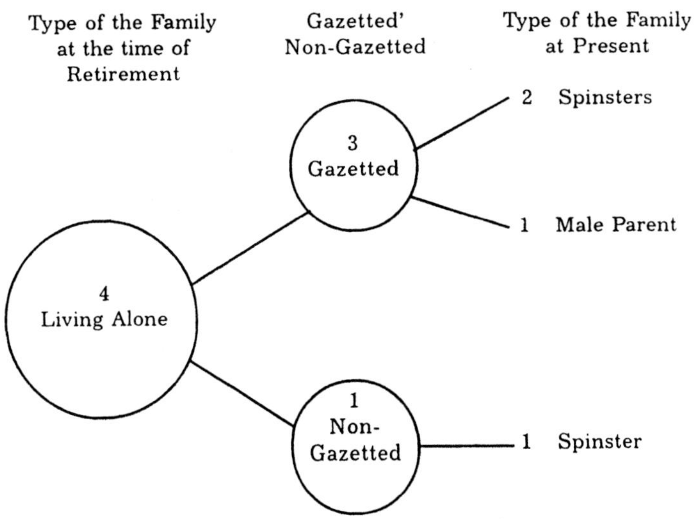

Digram 1-Showing continuity of Single-Member Domestic Units

Table 40. Percentage Distribution of the Present Previous Types at the time of

S. No.	Type of the family	Living alone		Incomplete nuclear family		Incomplete nuclear family with dependents		Complete nuclear family		complete nuclear family with dependents	
		G	NG	G	NG	G	NG	G	NG	G	NG
1.	Living alone	3	1	–	–	–	–	–	–	–	–
	Sub - Total	3	1	–	–	–	–	–	–	–	–
2.	Nuclear family										
	i. Incomplete nuclear family	–	–	18	17	–	–	2	–	–	–
	ii. Incomplete nuclear family with dependents	–	–	4	3	4	6	–	–	–	–
	iii. Complete nuclear families	2	1	4	3	–	–	21	28	–	–
	iv. Complete nuclear family with dependents	–	–	–		1	1	1	8	3	10
	Sub-Total	2	1	26	24	5	7	31	31	10	12
3.	Extended family										
	i. Incomplete vertically extended family	–	–	–	–	–	–	–	–	–	–
	ii. Complete vertically extended family	–	–	–	–	–	–	–	–	–	–
	iii. Complete horizontally extended family with dependents	–	–	–	–	–	–	–	–	–	–
	iv. Incomplete horizontally extended family	–	–	–	–	–	–	–	–	–	–
	v. Complete horizontally extended family	–	–	–	–	–	–	–	–	–	–
	vi. Complete horizontally extended family with dependents	–	–	–	–	–	–	–	–	–	–
	Sub-Total	–	–	–	–	–	–	–	–	–	–
	Grand Total	5 (2.5)	2 (1)	26 (13)	24 (12)	5 (2.5)	7 (3.5)	31 (15.5)	34 (15.5)	10 (5)	12 (6)

Present type of family

Note : G= Gazetted; NG=Non-gazetted
Figures in the paranthese indicate percentage

Type of Families after their Derivation from their Retirement of the Respondents

Incomplete vertically extended family		Complete vertically extended family		Complete vertically extended family with dependents		Incomplete horizontally extended family		Complete horizontally extended family		Complete horizontally extended family with dependents		Total
G	NG	G	NG	G	NG	G	NG	G	NG	G	NG	
–	–	–	–	–	–	–	–	–	–	–	–	4 (2)
–	–	–	–	–	–	–	–	–	–	–	–	4 (2)
–	–	–	–	–	–	–	–	–	–	–	–	37 (18.5)
–	–	–	–	–	–	–	–	–	–	–	–	17 (8.5)
–	–	–	–	–	–	–	–	–	–	–	–	59 (29.5)
12	–	–	–	–	–	–	–	–	–	–	–	36 (18)
–	–	–	–	–	–	–	–	–	–	–	–	149 (74.5)
–	–	–	–	2	1	–	–	–	–	–	–	13 (1.5)
–	–	13	12	1	1	–	–	–	–	–	–	27 (13.5)
–	–	–	–	1	1	–	–	–	–	–	–	1 2 (1)
–	–	–	–	–	–	–	–	2	1	–	–	3 (1.5)
–	–	–	–	–	–	–	–	3	6	–	–	9 (4.5)
–	–	–	–	–	–	–	–	1	2	–	–	3 (1.5)
–	–	13	12	4	3	–	–	6	9	–	–	47 (23.5)
–	–	13	12	4	3	–	–	6	9	–	–	200
–	–	(6.5)	(6)	(2)	(1.5)			(3)	(4.5)			(100)

Type of family at the time of retirement

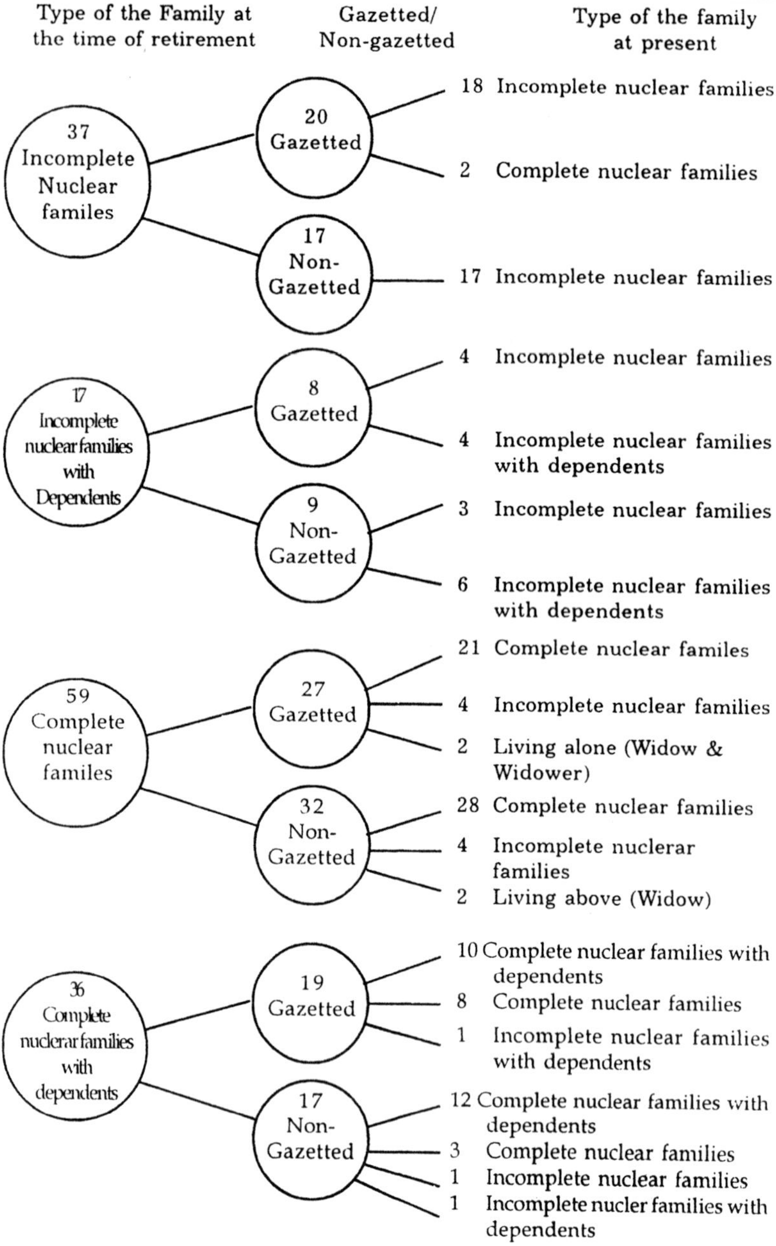

Dagram 2 : Showing continuity of and change in the Nuclear Families of the Respondents

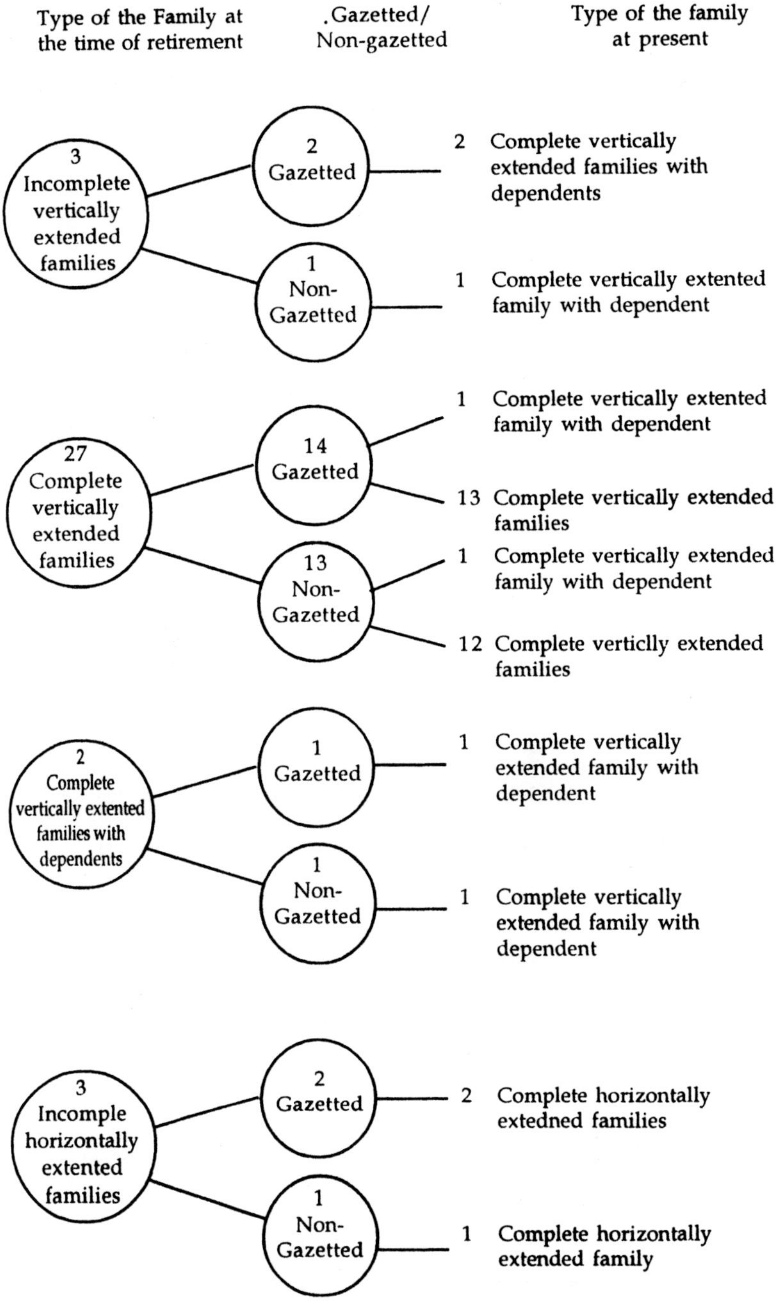

Type of the Family at the time of retirement
.Gazetted/ Non-gazetted
Type of the family at present
3 Incomplete vertically extended families
2 Gazetted
1 Non-Gazetted
2 Complete vertically extended families with dependents
1 Complete vertically extented family with dependent
27 Complete vertically extended families
14 Gazetted
13 Non-Gazetted
1 Complete vertically extented family with dependent
13 Complete vertically extended families
1 Complete vertically extended family with dependent
12 Complete verticlly extended families
2 Complete vertically extented families with dependents
1 Gazetted
1 Non-Gazetted
1 Complete vertically extended family with dependent
1 Complete vertically extended family with dependent
3 Incomple horizontally extented families
2 Gazetted
1 Non-Gazetted
2 Complete horizontally extedned families
1 Complete horizontally extended family

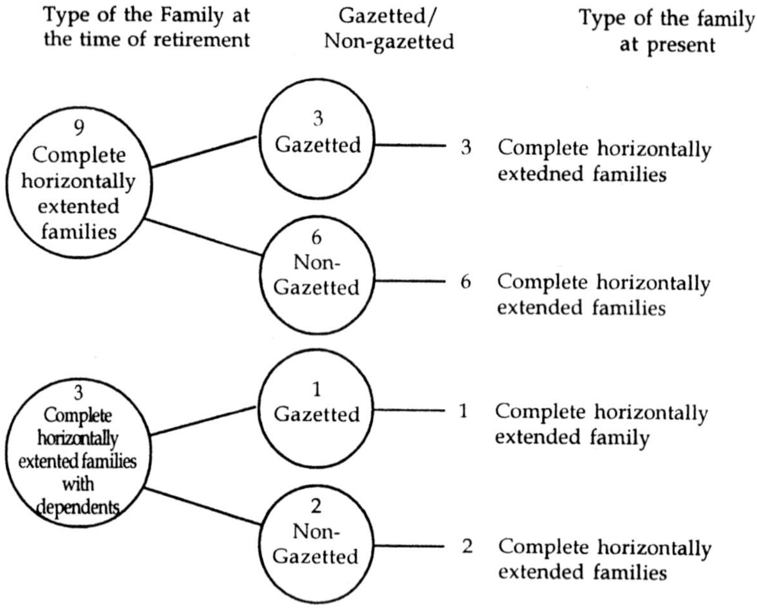

Dagram 2 : Showing continuity of and change in the nuclear families of the Respondents

Continuity of and change in single member domestic units:

There were 4 single member domestic units at the time of retirement. Now their number increased to 7. All the 4 respondents who were living alone at the time of retirement had taken a decision to live alone even after retirement for it was through such continuity of living they could expect social, economic and emotional support from relatives, manage their property with the help of their near relatives and have greater attention of a large number of kith and kin even in the last phase of their life. The other 3 single member domestic units formed only after retirement continue to be so even to this day because they too decided that living alone was the best solution for them to overcome the existing socio-economic constraints. The 4 single member domestic units continue to be so in the following manner.

i. S. Umadevi aged 65 years, is a spinster and retired as an officer in Railway Service. By virtue of her official position she had to move from place to place. So she did not have the opportunity to live with any one of her siblings who had established independent families. Having habituated to a lone life throughout her career in railways, she thought of continuing the same life even after retirement. She had already written a will specifying that all her property be given to the only son of her younger sister provided he takes care of her throughout her post-retirement life. Her younger sister's son visits her house now and then and helps her in many issues relating to property, pilgrimages and investment of savings in different banks. On some important festivals she visits her younger sister's house and spends a few days with her sister's family. Whenever she has some health trouble her younger sister and younger sister's son stay with her till she regains her normal health. Why she had preferred her younger sister's son to the children of her other siblings to be the heir of her property? She said that her younger sister's son is well educated, hard-working, intelligent and does not shirk from responsibilities. She observed the behaviour of the sons and daughters of all her siblings right from their childhood and of all those only her younger sister's son could come up to her expectations. Therefore, she prepared a will to give away all her property to her younger sister's son.

ii. The other two spinsters, aged 65 and 67 years respectively, were also single member domestic units at the time of their retirement. They decided to live alone for they were not financially in a good position and they had no reliable relatives to look after them. They said they have none to look after them except the people around them in their localities. So they have not taken any concrete decisions involving bequeathal of property or other such matters as in the previous case.

iii. At the time of retirement there was one male respondent who decided to live away from his wife and children. He continues to live alone even after retirement for he decided that that kind of living alone could help him have happiness and peaceful life till he leaves his mortal shell. He and also taken a decision in 1983 itself that unless he supports his wife and children he will not be fulfilling his duty towards his family. Therefore, he said that so long as he lives in this world, his prime responsibility as her the sacred texts is to fulfil his duties towards his family. For this reason he gives Rs. 1000 to his family every month for their maintenance. Whenever his children want some extra money he gives it on their request. Whenever, he is ill his wife comes to stay with him till he regains his normal health. He says that to implement his decisions it took almost four years between 1983 and 1986. His wife was reluctant to be away from him. When he could convince his wife, his children felt that to leave him alone was too bad on their part. When he assured them that he had the will power to keep himself aloof from the domestic life, his children too were prepared to leave him. However, his wife and his children visit him whenever they hear from him about their necessity. The children visit him she never they feel like seeing their father, wish to be with him on festival occasions, want to have some extra money for their expenses.

There were no widows or widowers who were living alone at the time of retirement. However, after retirement 3 complete nuclear families had broken giving rise to 3 single member domestic units of which 2 include widowers, one each among the gazetted and non-gazetted retirees, and 1 includes a widow among the gazetted retirees.

i. 2 individuals were living in complete nuclear families at the time of their retirement. Within three to five years after their retirement their spouses died on account of disease and accident. When their spouses pre-deceased them, troubles started in the family with regard to the division of the property among the children. They could not control their children from quarrelling and feuding with each other. They waited for a period of about two to three years expecting that their children would cease to quarrel amongst themselves and behave as real siblings. Their children, however, belied their hopes. Consequently, they established separate households for themselves. But regarding their properties all the three retirees have not taken any hard decision not to give away their properties to their children. They said that they would like to bequeath their properties to their children only a few days before their demise otherwise they will lose hold on their children.

ii. One individual among the gazetted retirees was living with husband and children at the time of retirement. Within 2 to 3 years after retirement, the retirees' husband pre-deceased her on account of disease. After a couple of months of this event children started quarelling with regard to who amongst them have to look after the widowed mother. This kind of conflict between her children resulted in frustration to her. Inspite of this mental trauma the widow continued to live with her children but in vain. Ultimately she decided to go away from her children and started living separately alone. She did not take any decision regarding distribution of her properties because the situation was not healthy to take any such decision as she may lose hold on her children.

Continuity of the change in incomplete nuclear families

There were only 37 incomplete nuclear families at the time of retirement which have increased to 50 after retirement, 26 among the gazetted and 24 among the non-gazetted retirees. Of the 50 incomplete nuclear families at present 35 were incomplete nuclear families, 7 were incomplete nuclear families with dependents, 7 were complete nuclear families and 1 was a complete nuclear family with dependents at the time of retirement. Thus 35 families at the time of retirement continued to be incomplete nuclear families even after retirement. These show certain similarities or differences as shown below:

i. 5 families, 2 among the gazetted and 3 among the non-gazetted retirees, were childless families at the time of retirement. Not having adopted any children all through their life they decided to lead the rest of their life in the same manner. The decision taken by these families are more or less similar. Mr. R. Shyama Prasad, aged 68, a retired teacher, says that he spent all his life with school children and his wife too filled the void of childlessness by coming to the school and spending her time amidst children and also enjoying with children who used to come to their house for tuition purposes. So, Shyama Prasad decided to bequeath his property to his brother's children and, also to his wife's sister's children.

ii. 3 families, 1 among the gazetted and 2 among the non-gazetted retirees, were complete nuclear families before their retirement. But a few years before retirement these families lost their only child because of accident and diseases. These retirees are now looked after by the retirees' brothers' children, sisters' children and the retirees' wives' brother's children and sisters' children to whom they decided to give away their property.

iii. 16 incomplete nuclear families, 10 among the gazetted and 6 among the non-gazetted retirees, have continued to be incomplete nuclear families even to this day. The situations and decisions that led to this condition is marriage of daughters. In accordance with the rules of patrilocality, daughters moved to their husbands' house. Hence all the 16 domestic groups could form into incomplete nuclear families over a period of two to five years between the time of retirement and the marriages of female children of the respondents.

iv. 8 families, 4 each among the gazetted and the non-gazetted, which were formed as residues after marriage of daughters and employment as well as marriage of sons continued to be incomplete nuclear even after retirement. After marriage daughters moved away in congruence with the rule of patrilocality. After their education, sons got employed at different places, some near to and some far away from Tirupati. Sons established their separate families. Daughters are living with their husbands. On festival and other occasions, sons and daughters visit their parents, stay for a few days, and return to their own families.

v. 3 families, one among the gazetted and 2 among the non-gazetted, continued to be incomplete nuclear families to this day. Prior to their retirement the respondents lost their female spouses. As a result, their families came to have themselves and their children. When some children came of age and were married, they were employed and they established their individual families at places of their employment. The unmarried children remained with their aged parents, the incompleteness of the families was only due to the death of female parent not due to the absence of some children who left the families after their marriage. The unmarried children remained in the house. Hence, the aged parent of the unmarried children together comprised incomplete unclear family. This composition remained unchanged to this day.

Of the remaining 15 incomplete nuclear families, 7 were incomplete nuclear families with dependents, another 7 were complete nuclear families and one was a complete nuclear family with dependents at the time of the retirement of the respondents. The following description shows how the transitions of these families occurred after the retirement of the respondents.

i. 2 families, one each among the gazetted retirees and non-gazetted retirees, were incomplete nuclear families at the time of retirement. Each of them included a man; his wife and his wife's unmarried sister who was a dependent. Wife's sister's marriage was celebrated two years after retirement. Therefore, the family became an incomplete nuclear family. The couple took decision to give their property only to those who look after them in the last phase of their life. Therefore, the couple's near relatives like husband's brothers and wife's brothers are now paying some attention to the couple in matter property to only one of the women's brothers because he is helping the couple in economic, social and emotional matters as per the wish of the couple.

ii. 5 families, 3 among the gazetted and 2 among the non-gazetted, were incomplete nuclear families with dependents at the time of retirement of respondents. Each of them included a man, his wife and his dependent namely wife's sister's daughter, who was prospecting her college education. Between three and five years after retirement, the dependent left for her natal home. Subsequently the family became an incomplete nuclear family. Thus all the five families of this type are derivatives from the incomplete nuclear families with dependents. The couple in the five incomplete nuclear families now and then procure help from near relatives and friends in the management of their real estates and during their illness.

iii. 7 families, 4 among the gazetted and 3 among the non-gazetted retirees, were complete nuclear families at the time of retirement. Each one of them included a man, his wife and his unmarried daughters. Within three to five years after their retirement, each employee conducted the marriage of their daughters. Consequently the aged couple in each family comprised an incomplete nuclear family. The sons-in-law and daughters after visit them to give them the needed social and emotional support besides some economic support whenever required. The retirees say that their sons-in-law are helping them in the way that sons help their fathers.

iv. One family among the non-gazetted was a complete nuclear family with dependents at the time of retirement. This family comprised a couple, unmarried children and the widowed father-in-law of the retiree. The children got married in a period of about 3 to 5 years after retirement and moved out of Tirupati. Along with one of the married son, the widowed father-in-law of the retiree too went away leaving the original family as an incomplete nuclear one.

Continuity of and change in incomplete nuclear family with dependents

There were 17 incomplete nuclear families with dependent at the time of retirement but their number has come down to 12, 5 among the gazetted and 7 among the non-gazetted retirees, after the retirement of the respondents. Ten families, 4 from the gazetted and 6 from the non-gazetted have continued to be in complete nuclear with dependents till to day as the dependents still cling to these families.

There are 10 families, 4 from the gazetted and 6 from the non-gazetted retirees, which have continued to be incomplete nuclear with dependents even after retirement. The following description accounts for the continuity of these ten families:

i. 2 families, one each from the gazetted and non-gazetted retirees, continue to be incomplete nuclear with dependents as the dependents who are the retirees' wives' unmarried sisters continued to live with these families. They are of great help to these families in terms of providing some assistance in household work such as kitchen work, sweeping the court yard, cleaning the utensils, washing the clothes, accompanying the retirees and their spouses to market, cinema halls, recreation centres and temples.

ii. 4 families, 2 each from the gazetted and non-gazatted retirees, retained the same family structure even after retirement because the dependents who were the retirees' wives' sisters' daughters continue to stay on with these families. These dependents are still college going girls and are yet to complete their education in Tirupati. Therefore, the families continued to be incomplete nuclear with dependents.

iii. 4 families, 1 among the gazetted and 3 among the non-gazetted respondents, continued to be incomplete nuclear with dependents. A few years before their retirement the respondents arranged the marriages of their children. Subsequently their children were employed elsewhere and established their individual families. Meanwhile, some distant relatives joined the respondents' familes as dependents. Therefore, the respondents' families became incomplete nuclear with dependents. These families continued to be incomplete nuclear with dependents for the dependents who are distant relatives of these families clinged to these families as they have no other relatives to look after them.

There are 2 incomplete nuclear families with dependents which are actually the transistions of the complete nuclear families with dependents. The following depiction reveals how these families acquired their present structure.

i. One family among the gazetted was complete nuclear with dependents before the retirement of the respondents. The family consisted of a man, his wife, his son and his father's widowed elder sister who was a dependent. His father's widowed elder sister had three sons who were well educated and employed at New Delhi, Lucknow and Calcutta. She chose to be a dependent on her youngest son employed at Cultutta and therefore she was staying at Calcutta for some time. However, the environment at Calcutta was not conductive to her health. Then she tried her best to live as a dependent of her other sons at New Delhi and Lucknow. Neither at New Delhi nor at Lucknow she could keep up good health. So her nephew at Tirupati decided to take care of his aunt in her old age and he started giving her all the required medical and personal services. All this happened two years before retirement of the respondent. Therefore, at the time of retirement his family consisted of himself, his wife, his unmarried son and his father's sister who was an aged widow. Three years after his retirement his son got married and established a separate family at the place of his employment at Hyderabad. Consequently the retiree's family included himself, his wife, his father's sister who is a widow. This composition of his family has not changed in the last five years.

ii. One family from the non-gazetted employees was also a complete nuclear family with dependents at the time of the retirement. His family included himself, his wife, his unmarried daughter and his wife's widowed elder sister who was more than 55 years. Within three years after his retirement his daughter completed her post-graduation and got employed in a local college. Thereafter, he performed the marriage of his daughter with his father's sister's son, who was a well placed employee drawing a fat salary. After his daughter's marriage his family included himself, his wife and his dependent namely his wife's elder sister who is a widow. His wife's elder sister continues to be a dependent because she has none to look after her with care and affection except her sister and her sister's husband.

Continuity of the change in complete nuclear families

There were 59 complete nuclear families at the time of retirement of the respondents. But after retirement, the respondents came to have 62 complete nuclear families, 31 each from the gazetted and the non-gazetted categories. Among these 62 families, 49 continued to be complete nuclear even after retirement, 2 incomplete nuclear families changed into complete nuclear after retirement, and 11 complete nuclear families with dependents changed into complete nuclear families after retirement. Thus continuity can be seen with reference to 49 domestic units and changed with regard to 13 domestic units to be complete nuclear families in the post-retirement life of the respondents. The discussion focuses its attention how the domestic units continued to be complete nuclear families.

i. 11 families, 4 from the gazetted and 7 from the non-gazetted, continued to include a couple and their unmarried sons. As the sons are not still old enough to get married and many of them are still in their education these families remained as complete nuclear. These retirees are aspiring that their children should get more higher education and reach creditable positions in the field of employment.

ii. 5 families, 2 from the gazetted and 3 from the non-gazetted retirees, included each a man, his wife and his unmarried daughter at the time of retirement of the respondents. One or two years before their retirement some respondents arrange the marriages of their daughters. Thus even after their retirement, the respondents continued to maintain complete nuclear families as the latter were left with unmarried daughters. Even though the retirees felt the pinch of seeing the unmarried condition of their daughters they are comfortable when they receive all the help from their employed daughters. Some of the retirees are getting their daughters educated and some are waiting for the examination results of their daughter. Most of these retirees are seriously thinking of the marriages of their daughters. These daughters were left back in the family after elder daughters left their natal homes soon after getting married.

iii. 33 families, 15 among the gazetted and 18 among the non-gazetted, were complete nuclear at the time of retirement of the employees. Each one of them included a man, his wife and his sons and daughters were married and left their natal homes to establish their own families, the unmarried sons and daughters remained at natural homes. All this happened after retirement of the employees. Now, among the unmarried children in these families, some of the sons and daughters have just finished their college education and are appearing in competitive examinations and some of them are still in their education. These children look after their aged parents in addition to prosecuting their education and career. Married children visit their old parents and unmarried siblings whenever they wish to see them.

There are 13 families, 10 from the gazetted and 3 from the non-gazetted, which have transformed into complete nuclear families after retirement. The conditions which have led to the change are depicted as follows:

i. 2 families, one each among the gazetted and non-gazeted retirees, became complete nuclear families after the dependent sisters of the retirees were married and moved out. These sisters were the youngest sisters of the retirees and it took about 4 to 6 years for the retirees to get these marriages arranged. In the money allotted to their children's career, the retirees had to use a part of it for these marriages as these dependents were totally dependent on their brothers.

ii. One family among the gazetted retirees became complete nuclear after the only dependent that is the widowed father-in-law of the retiree passed away. The widowed father-in-law was an octogenarian and died of old age. There were no serious setbacks in the family due to the death of this dependent.

iii. One family among the gazetted retirees became complete nuclear after the widowed mother-in-law of the retiree died. This unhappy event, however, altered the rest of the structure of the family. The widowed mother-in-law was bedridden for a long time and she was now and then saying that death was better to her then lying on the bed and suffering from bed sores and other problems.

iv. One family among the gazetted retirees became compete nuclear after the retiree's sister's husband passed away due to old age. The dependent was suffering from heart problem and heart attack is the cause of the death. He was a dependent on this family after his wife passed away.

v. 4 of these, 3 among the gazetted and 1 among the non-gazetted retirees, became complete nuclear families after the child of the son or daughter of the retirees went away after completing his or her education. There were no further educational courses for these dependents to continue at their grand parents' place. So they have taken a decision to send their grand-children to places where they could get further chances to continue their career.

vi. One family among the gazetted retirees became complete nuclear with the couple and a child after the dependent who is a widowed mother-in-law passed away in her old age at 80 years.

vii. One family from the gazetted retirees became complete

nuclear after the maternal grandmother died who was a dependent till that moment.

viii. One family from the non-gazetted retirees became complete nuclear when the widowed father of the retiree passed away due to cancer. This caused a little setback to the retiree as he had a long attachment to his father since the retiree's childhood. So the retiree decided to name one of his grandchildren after his father.

ix. One family from the gazetted retirees became complete nuclear with the retiree's son joining the family after completing his education elsewhere and after the widowed father-in-law died when on a pilgrimage.

Continuity of and change in complete nuclear families with dependents

There were 36 complete nuclear families with dependents at the time of retirement of the respondents. Their number has came down to 22 at present, which have 10 from the gazetted and 12 from the non-gazetted retirees. In other words, only 22 of the 36 complete nuclear families with dependents continued their structure and the remaining 14 have changed into other types of families. The description given below shows how the 22 complete nuclear families with dependents have acquired their present structure.

i. 8 families, 5 from the gazetted and 3 from the non-gazetted retirees continued to be complete nuclear with dependents as the widowed fathers and mothers stayed on with these families. The retires and the dependents are quite happy in these families, hence and dependents continued to be members of these families.

ii. One family from the gazetted retirees continued to be complete nuclear with dependents as the retiree's elder brother continued to stay with the same family who wished to breath his last in the presence of all his relatives in the family.

iii. 2 families, one each from the gazetted and non-gazetted retirees, continued to maintain the same familial structure as the retirees' widowed elder sisters stayed on with the same family as they were too old to go any where and also the retirees' family members relished the presence of these dependents.

iv. 2 families, one each from the gazetted and non-gazetted categories, continued to be complete nuclear with dependents as the retirees' wives' widowed elder sisters were members of these families to date. These dependents are very helpful to the retirees' wives and have given away whetever little properties they had to these families and have decided to live till their last in these families.

v. 2 families from the non-gazetted retirees continued to be complete nuclear with dependents when the widowed father-in-law of the retirees who are octogenarians stayed on with these families and did decide to breath their last in Tirumala which is only20 kilometres away from Tirupati. They wished so, as Tirumala is the holy seat of Lord Venkateswara, a Hindu God considered as incarnation of Lord Vishnu.

vi. 2 families, one each from the gazetted and non-gazetted retirees, remained as complete nuclear with dependents as the widowed mothers-in-law of the retirees wanted to lead the rest of their lives in their eldest daughters homes and so these families maintained the same familial composition before and after retirement.

vii. 2 families, one each from the gazetted and non-gazetted retirees, continued to be complete nuclear with dependents as the distant relatives attached to these families as dependents could not go anywhere as there were none to look after these dependents. So these retirees have more or less took similar decisions to take care for these dependents.

viii. One family from the non-gazetted category maintained the same composition as the father's sister in the family remained as dependent on the family as she was disabled and is under the medical supervison of an orthopaedician in Tirupati.

ix. 2 families from the non-gazetted retirees continued to maintain the same structure as the eldest daughters' sons of the retirees continued their education staying in these families. As Tirupati is a big educational center these families have decided to keep these grand children inTirupati and get them educated.

x. One family among the non-gazetted retirees continued to be complete nuclear with dependents as the grandson of the retiree continued to stay as a member of this family as he is doing his first year engineering graduation in Tirupati where he could secure a seat successfully passing through the entrance examination. Even though there are hostel facilities the retiree wanted his grandson to stay in his house and complete his educational course thereby giving him all the parental affection and care.

Continuity of and Change in extended families:

There were 47 extended families of which 3 were incomplete vertically extended, 27 were complete vertically extended, 2 were complete vertically extended with dependents, 3 were incomplete horizontally extended, 9 were complete horizontally extended and 3 were complete horizontally extended families with dependents. The number of extended families has neither increased nor decreased. It has remained the same before and after retirement. However, of the 47 extended families, 36 continued their structures and the remaining 11 acquired new structures and in the process, 3 incomplete vertically extended, 3 incomplete horizontally extended and 3 complete horizontally extended families with dependents, and 2 complete vertically extended families have given rise to new structure and the rest maintained their structures at the time of retirement of the respondents.

Continuity of and change in complete vertically extended families

There are now only 25 complete vertically extended families, 13 are from the gazetted and 12 are from the non-gazetted retirees. There were 27 complete vertically extended families at the time of retirement. But 2 families one each from the gazetted and non-gazetted retirees transformed into complete vertically extended families with dependents.

i. 12 families, 6 each from the gazetted and non-gazetted categories continued to the complete vertically extended families before and after retirement as the sons of these retirees continued their employment in Tirupati itself. As these retirees needed emotional, financial and physical support from their childrens' families these complete vertically extended families have not altered their structures.

ii. 13 families, 7 from the gazetted and 6 from the non-gazetted, have continued the same family composition for more or less the same reasons as explained with reference to the continuity of complete vertically extended families. These retirees' have several sons. But some were living away from Tirupati and were visiting their parents on all important occasions like festivals and socio-religious functions. So, even after some married sons established their separate families one of the married sons continued to live with his parents. This situation resulted in the formation of complete vertically extended families. So these families has retained their composition that existed at the time of retirement of the respondents.

Continuity of and change in the complete vertically extended families with dependents

There were only 2 complete vertically extended families with dependents at the time of retirement which have increased to 7, 4 from the gazetted and 3 from the non-gazetted categories.

i. 2 families, one each from the gazetted and non-gazetted categories, remained complete vertically extended families with dependents before and after retirement. The dependents are retirees' daughter's daughters in one family and daughter's son in the other family. As these grandchildren have to be educated in Tirupati because of non-availability of standard educational institutions at their place, they continued to stay on with these families. The expenditure incurred for the dependent in the gazetted retiree's family is borne by the retiree's family whereas it is not the case in the non-gazetted retirees' family.

There are 5 families, 3 from the gazetted and 2 from the non-gazetted retirees, which changed into complete vertically extended families with dependents. The following explanation clearly depicts how the transition took place.

i. 3 families, 2 from the gazetted and 1 from the non-gazetted retirees, which were incomplete vertically extended families became complete vertically extended families with dependents in a period of 3 to 5 years after retirement. Two families from the gazetted acquired this structure on bearing grandchildren and on incorporating the dependents like widowed mother and father of the retirees.

ii. 2 families, one each from the gazetted and non-gazetted became complete vertically extended families with dependents after 2 to 4 years from retirement. They were complete vertically extended families before or at the time of retirement. The widowed sister of the gazetted retiree and the widowed mother of the non-gazetted retiree joined these families due to ill-health. The financial position of these dependents was also grim and there was no other alternative except to accept to be dependents on the families of these retirees.

Continuity of and change in horizontally extended families

There were 9 complete horizontally extended families at the time of retirement which have increased to 15, 6 among the gazetted and 9 among the non-gazetted retirees. The increase as stated earlier, is due to the transition of 3 incomplete horizontally extended families and 3 complete vertically extended families with dependents into complete horizontally extended families.

9 families, 3 from the gazetted and 6 from the non-gazetted respondents, have continued to be complete horizontally extended families before and after retirement. These families have not changed their composition as they have decided to live in the same style because such a living was considered as a safe contrivance for meeting the growing expenditure. Some of these families, though do not share a common hearth, live in separate houses in a big compound which they inherited from their forefathers.

There are 6 families, 3 each from the gazetted and non-gazetted categories, which have changed into complete horizontally extended families. The following description highlights the facts and conditions that have led to the transformation.

i. 3 families, 2 from the gazetted and 1 from the non-gazetted, which were incomplete horizontally extended families became complete horizontally extended families as the brothers' families bore children within a period of a year or two after retirement.

ii. 3 families, 1 from the gazetted and two from the non-gazetted, which were complete horizontally extended families with dependents have changed into complete horizontally extended families as the paternal grandparents in these families either died or moved out to elsewhere, hence the change in the structure of these families.

WORKING OF THE FAMILY

Inter-personal relations

The inter-personal relations in the families of the retirees present a picture of tradition and modernity. On the one hand, socio-cultural conditions or circumstances influenced men and women in the roles and actions they deemed appropriate or worthy at different stages of their life course within their families. On the other hand modern education, employment, industrialization and urbanization have influenced men and women, husband and wives, parents and children to adapt their roles to the extent they can to the changing social, cultural and economic domain. Formal schooling or education, employment and economic background acquired early in life have instilled knowledge and skills, self-confidence, self-esteem and competence, a breadth of perspective and intellectual aptitude for abstract planning.

The retirees belong to different castes and sub-castes. However, all the castes and sub-castes have uniform rules in terms of patriarchy, patriliny and patrilocality. The rules of patriarchy contain a male authority line headed by the eldest male unless he has passed the responsibility on to his inheriting son. The family name and property are transmitted down the male line. According to the rules of patriliny ancestry is always traced through male line. As per the rules of patrilocality the wife leaves her family at a given stage of the marriage ritual and joins the family of her husband, who then insists that he meet her obligations. The rights of a husband are claimed uniformly in all the castes and sub-castes.

As per rules of patriarchy, patriliny and patrilocality people recruit wives for their sons through careful match-making, ensuring the best arrangement for the new unit, as well as for the family of the future husband and wife. The women's family provides a dowry to help set up house-keeping. The unit is maintained with the help of an institutionalized division of labour. Children are filiated to the line of male parent. The foliation leads not only to the activation of many kinship roles such as grand-children, nieces, nephews, grand-parents, aunts, uncles, and so forth, but also to guarantee of the proper arrangements for marriage and for inheritance when so designated.

As all the castes and sub-castes exercise similar rules of patriarchy, patriliny and patrilocality they try to mould their young in a way which is almost uniform. As a result all people, irrespective of their caste or sub-caste status, become almost similar social persons in terms of similar processes of enculturation. In this kind of the cultural frame of the respondents not only the rights and duties of spouses, offspring, siblings and so on but also the processes of enculturation are almost uniform.

Husbands and wives in the family

The relations of aged couples revolve round the differential authority of the aged husbands and the invariable submissive and hard-working nature of the aged wives.

One of the important factors in the family after retirement of husband is the presence of husband for longer hours in the house. However, the reaction of wives to husbands longer presence in the house is not uniform in all families. Care taken by wives after retirement of their husbands remained unchanged in almost 68 percent of the cases. Nearly 25 percent of the sample respondents have indicated of spouse taking more care after retirement. One of the reasons given by the wives to account for this factor is the ill-health of the retirees. Other important reasons given is that husbands are spend-thrifts and also the wife wants to avoid loneliness by her husband's presence in the house.

Mr. A Narasimha Murthy, a retired non-gazetted officer from Andhra Pradesh State Service, aged 69, says that he is a diabetic and has the problem of low blood pressure. These problems are increasing along with age and so the respondent is dependent on his wife for major routine activities as these health problems are troubling him frequently. So the retiree says that his wife taking care after him has increased after retirement owing to ill-health. He further says, "My wife will be accompanying me whenever I go for entertainment like cinema, musical concerts and also to temples." So the dependency on wife has stretched even to activities outside his house.

So, it may be taken into account that retirement does not create large impact so far as wife's care towards her husband is concerned.

Among the wives some are not particular whether the husbands stay in or out. A few are in different to the presence of their husbands in the house. There is a clear-cut-seggregation of husband-wife roles in such families.

In extended families the relationship between old couples is put in a disadvantageous position. In this context, many factors like loss in status, presence of old couples as a curtailment of freedom of other members have bearing on the relationship of the aged couples.

The economic and social activities of the husband and wife are regulated by a division of labour which is not as clear-cut as it was in their younger age. The aged woman assists her husband in his daily routine in many ways. In terms of tradition this is recognized as a sacred job of the wife. In the early morning hours of the day she supplies water to him to complete his morning ablutions. In all the families it is observed that the aged couples are the first to wake up in the family and complete all morning chores.

Before breakfast the aged husband goes out for fetching vegetables and milk. After this he worships the household deities. His wife arranges all the paraphernalia necessary for the worship. After completing the worship, he is served breakfast. In cases where the wife is ill and cannot assist her husband and in turn takes all the help from her husband the situation is just the opposite. The following case study will illustrate this. Mr. R. Sampath Kumar, aged 62, a retired gazetted officer from Andhra Pradesh Secretariat, says his wife is bedridden two years after his retirement and since then he assists his wife in her daily routine and also recites mythological texts to his wife.

After breakfast the husband spends some time in reading newspaper, listening to morning radio or reviewing the breakfast television programmes. About 35 percent of the sample families have television sets. At this time, the wife spends some time with the daughter-in-law in helping her grand-children get ready for school. All these activities are performed before ten O' clock in the morning.

After 10 O' clock in the morning, the husband who is a retiree takes up minor jobs like paying grandchildren's school fees and electricity bills, visiting close friends and relatives and attending to pensioners association activities. During this time the aged wife helps her daughter-in-law in kitchen activities like cooking food for lunch and supervising the servant-maid in washing the clothes and cleaning the utensils.

If the aged husband is doing a post-retirement job, his activities become different from those of the other retirees. Around 9 O' clock the aged husbands go to their respective work places either by walk or by rickshaw, bus, moped, scooter or motor cycle depending upon the physical proximity of the office to home.

At the time of taking lunch or supper at home couples may or may not sit together. In a little more than 57 percent of the families the couples sit together and dine. In about 43 percent of the families the couple are traditional. The aged wife and daughter-in-law sit together for food after the head of the family completes his lunch. The remaining are not particular about this practice. At lunch the aged couple share good moods regarding the preparations and other things. The wife serves her husband the cooked items, keeping in mind his diet requirements.

The wife offers to her husband pieces of betelnut and a few betel leaves smeared with optimum quantity of 'lime' (sunnam). Her husband leisurely chews them. A few minutes relaxation on an easy-chair or armchair helps them feel free to have a nap on the bed. Almost all the aged respondents have expressed their inevitability of going through this post-lunch nap.

At bed-time the aged couples spend their time with their grand-children by narrating them either tales from the epics or certain more stories and guiding them in their home-work given in the school. Discussing the family matters with their sons take place at nights, some time after supper and before going to bed.

Parents and children in the family

Like the young parents, the aged parents also dream of the betterment of their children, and parents who do otherwise are widely talked about in this respect.

A sort of formal relations exist between the aged parents and children even if they love each other greatly. These features in the relationship may be attributed to super-ordination-subordination connections between aged parents and children.

Among the aged parents both the gazetted and non-gazetted

retirees are prepared to invest their money and efforts in the development and growth of their children. Present investigation reveals that many of them have even sacrificed their personal comforts and gratifications to provide higher education to their children. That the children would look after the needs of their parents is taken by them as a normal duty of the sons just as the parents regard themselves responsible for the education and marriage of their children even when they have been retired from the jobs.

The parents arrange the marriages of their sons and daughters. They pay dowries to their daughters but receive dowries for their sons. In 57 percent of the cases, the sons were married earlier than the daughters because the dowries received from the sons are to some extent spent on the marriage of their daughters. In 18 percent of the cases, sons and daughters are simultaneously married. This pattern is more or less the same in both the gazetted and non-gazetted categories. Here, the dowries received for sons are spent at the same time for the marriage of daughters. In 15 percent of the cases, parents-in-law not only provided dowries but also secured them jobs. Such an arrangement has helped the retirees to overcome major socio-economic crises, that is, arranging the marriage of grown up sons and daughters and putting the grown-up sons in one job or the other. In the remaining cases, dowries were avoided because they were exchange marriages. A few cases were love-marriages of which a case is based on the consent of the parents of both the boy and the girl.

Table- 41 reveals about the decisions taken in extended families among the retirees. A total of 48 families in both the gazetted and non-gazetted are living in extended families. The table reveals the fact whether the head of the family (the respondent) or all in the extended family or children alone take decisions in case of a number of family matters.

It is clear from the above table that more non-gazetted than gazetted retirees take decisions in family matters, consulting one another. Taking decisions by mutual consent is a very healthy indicator of an extended family. Taking into consideration the above indicator it may be said that more number of the extended families among the non-gazetted are much integrated than those of the gazetted. This may be attributed to the fact that the non-gazetted are of the view that security for an extendd family can be obtained

Table 41. Distribution of the families of the Retirees according to the Decisions taken in Extended Families

Sl. No.	Family matter	Gazetted Retirees			Non-gazetted Retirees			Total
		Self	All in the family	Children	Self	All in the family	Children	
1.	Education of children	10	5	4	3	10	15	47
		Chi-square value = 10.5927 (Significant at 1% level)						
2.	Marriage of children and grand-children	6	13	-	5	20	3	47
		Chi-square value = 1.2208 (Not Significant)						
3.	Participation in caste and other functions	2	8	9	8	12	8	47
		Chi-square value = 2.6068 (Not Significant)						
4.	Exchange of gifts among relatives	3	12	4	4	14	10	47
		Chi-square value = 0.9502 (Not Significant)						
5.	Visiting relatives and in-laws of the children	4	10	5	6	18	4	47
		Chi-square value = 0.8213 (Not Significant)						
6.	Purchase of property	4	13	2	9	11	8	47
		Chi-square value = 3.3378 (Not Significant)						
7.	Construction of houses	6	12	1	10	13	5	47
		Chi-square value = 0.5834 (Not Significant)						
8.	Disposal of property	8	11	-	10	10	8	47
		Chi-square value = 0.0911 (Not Significant)						
9.	Holding of family functions and ceremonies	4	14	1	8	10	10	47
		Chi-square value = 7.6526 (Significant at 5% level)						
		47	98	26	63	118	71	

by possessing wider consensus. This consensus action takes part while deciding family matters. Many of the gazetted retirees are less bothered about the security of their extended families as they are financially sound than the non-gazetted. The respondents who feel their sons are immature and inexperienced, also hold key over family matters and decision making.

Mr. R.S. Naidu who has retired as a gazetted officer from Tirumala Tirupati Devasthanams says: "My elder son, though employed cannot manage family affairs and is immature to take decisions regarding children's education." As a result the older person took up the responsibility and leads the family. The control of the older person is such that if one aspect of family matters is handed over to him he tries to pervade through all other aspects and holds key to all the family matters and takes decision alone. This is the case with Mr. R.S. Naidu. In the same way as Mr. R.S. Naidu, one more retiree holds total responsibility in an extended family which includes himself, he has saved a good amount of money in his service and is now able to extend financial help to his son and hence control over the family.

Education of children is one area where children alone take decisions among the non-gazetted in more number because the child in the non-gazetted category is more educated than the father and knows better than the parent to shape his future..

Significantly more number among the non-gazetted take decisions regarding marriage of children and grand-children, sitting together. This is one area where it is evident that the extended family of the non-gazetted retiree is more interested and shows a flair for the smooth functioning of the extended family. Visiting of relatives and in-laws of the children, participation in caste and other functions, and exchange of gifts among relatives are matters of family interests where more non-gazetted than gazetted retirees take decisions consulting all the family members. In all the above matters it is clear that decision taken by all in the family is an indicator of how well-knit are the extended families and this integration is a result of the security of the individual in an extended family.

Decisions regarding purchase of property, construction of houses, disposal of property and holding of family functions and ceremonies are family matters where the differences between the gazetted and the non-gazetted retirees as to who take decisions, are of significance. As regards the above matters, reasonable member of families in both the gazetted and non-gazetted categories of retirees take decisions by mutual consultation with one another. Purchase of property and construction of hoses are the most vital matters for any family. So far as decision making is concerned there is not much of a significant difference between the gazetted and the non-gazetted retirees in the above matters.

It can be summed up by seeing the indications in Table-41 that there are less significant differences between gazetted and non-gazetted as far as decision-making is concerened.

In extended families the relations between parents and children are by and large cordial. Sons and daughters are not sufficiently removed from their emotional and other forms of dependency on the parents. They support their parents and thereby discharge their duties as protectors of their aged parents. In families where some children got settled and others continue to depend on the employed children, the older person continues to hold authority and control as the employed child does not care for the rest of the family.

L. Seetharama Murthy, aged 66, is a retired teacher. He lives with three sons and a daughter. His eldest son got a job and does not care for the rest. So it is indispensablke for the retired father to hold responsibility and see that his children eat and live with at least bare necessities.

If parents live separately from their adult children who had established their own families of procreation elsewhere, they visit their children's families now and then and come back. Sometimes, they may stay for about two months if the married children require them for some assistance. The parents give three major reasons for their desire to live alone, or, at least, not to move into the household of a married son: a wish for independence, a wish to avoid strain or possibly conflict in their relations with offspring and their families, and a wish to avoid work being imposed upon.

The detailed reasons focus on the importance that many parents attach to maintaining their own household within which they can organize their time and work, they can decide when and what to eat, rather than adjusting to the decisions of daughters-in-law. They do not enjoy the idea of being peripheral to the life in another home which has operated without them for some time. Some are uncomfortable with their children's friends, neighbours and neighbourhoods. Many aged parents are accustomed to a lower economic life style than now led by their children, thanks to the help they had given them in earlier years.

The possibility of strain with the children and their families is given as an important reason why some retirees do not want to live with them if they can be economically independent and well enough to keep their own residence. Visits or occasional extended stay with adult children make evident the possibility for such a strain. Parents are accustomed to observing and commenting on the behaviour of their children and grand-children, but their comments are not always welcome, especially when they are seen as criticism or attempts to control.

The cultural changes since the parents' days of youth, and the unwillingness of modern parents to use old fashioned methods in bringing up children or running a home often lead to strong differences of opinion. Besides, the sons and daughters-in-law are embedded in a web of relations which the parents may find unsatisfactory or which can produce adverse reactions to their presence and behaviour. The son and his wife may be willing to put up with the advice of the parents but the aged parents know very well that the son and daughter-in-law have no tolerance. Retirees are afraid that they will not be able to desist from actions that may make them look like interfering or as undersirable house-mates, causing problems with daughter-in-law and perhaps with grand-children.

Finally, retirees are seen often happy with their lighter workload. They fear that work will be imposed upon them by their children, if they move into the busy house-hold of their children. They object to more baby-sitting as opposed to grand-parenting which involve enculturation of grand children. They do not want to do house-work while the younger people enjoy themselves.

Children living away from the natal home are seen several times a year. Daily contact occurs with the offspring who live in the same street or in some other street within the town. Not all sons or daughters who live in the neighbourhood are seen daily but on an average several times a week or once in a week.

Grand-parent and grand-child in the family

The relations between grand-parents and their grand-children can be distinguished by mutual affection and aid. Whenever they meet they joke with each other. The grand-parents and grand-children some times joke to the extent of teasing each other. The grand-parents narrate some myths and legends, render ancient and modern stories and interpret riddles to their grand-children. Also the grand-parents help their grand-children in completing the latter's home-work assigned at school, and also make all the grand children and the grand children's friends sit and give them coaching in their respective subjects and prepare them for the class tests and unit tests conducted by the school authorities.

Grand-children are not only enjoyed but also make the grand-parents feel like important, respected and useful persons.

The grand-children are expected to help their grand-parents in matters of social, physical, economic and emotional support. The present enquiry reveals that only 13 percent of the grand-children help their grand-parents. What is the reason for this low percentage? It is found that the relation between grand-children and grand-parents provides intense enjoyment for only a brief time while the grand-children are little, and that the generation drift apart when the grand-children become strongly involved in their own lives. Since most of the retirees are between 59 and 70 years, their grand-children are either little to provide any substantial support or in the midst of the expanding stage of their own family and thus unavailable to the grand-parents for social, economic, emotional and other supports.

Table-42 shows the percentage distribution of the retirees according to their dependence on children. There is not much difference between the retirees who answered that dependence is unavoidable and dependence is avoidable.

Figures in the Table–42 reveal that a near equal number of retirees were feeling that dependence is unavoidable and avoidable. Here again more non-gazetted were feeling that they unavoidably depended on their children. This is indicative of the economic insecurity among the non-gazetted retirees. But the same economic insecurity is seen even among a considerable in number of the gazetted.

Table 42. Percentage Distribution of the Retirees according to their Dependence on Children

S.No.	Dependence	Number of Gazetted Retirees	Number Non-gazetted Retirees	Total
1.	Dependence is unavoidable	43	61	104
2.	Dependence is avoidable	57	39	96
	Total	100	100	200 (100%)

Chi-square value = 6.4907 (Significant at 1% level)

TYPES OF FAMILIAL ADJUSTMENT

Bases of familial adjustment

According to Schneiders, adjustment is a process involving both mental and behavioural responses by which an individual strives to cope with inner needs, tensions, frustrations and conflicts, and tries to bring harmony between these inner demands and those imposed upon him by the world in which he lives (Schneiders 1965). However, Kuhlen conceives adjustments both as a process and as a state, and this distinction is appropriate as it provides an insight into the dynamics of adjustment phenomenon (Kuhlen 1959: 852)

Adjustment to aging and retirement can be conceived as an individual's restructuring of attitudes and behaviour in response to a new situation in such a way as to integrate the expression of his aspiration with the expectation and demands of society (Cavan 1949:11).

After retirement or at the time of approaching retirement choices are narrowed down in terms of family types. One has to adjust to the newly emerging family conditions. The way the retirees adjusted or shaped themselves or result in breaking away into separate families. The patterns of familial adjustment as practiced by the retirees show some interesting facts.

An attempt is made here to extract the different patterns of family adjustment of the retirees on the basis of the retirees' approach to the family problems. Accordingly we will have three broad classes of retirees:

i. Those getting adjusted to living alone:

ii. Those getting adjusted to living with other family members with sustained independency; and

iii. Those getting adjusted to living with other family members with dependency factors associated.

Pattern adjustment to living alone

Retirees who got adjusted to living alone come under this pattern of living. In a way this pattern of living reduced the mental tensions of the retirees because this gave them association with no one. Widows, widowers, spinsters and those who lost interest in marital life come under this category.

This pattern of adjustment reveals independence in several socio-economic matters. Economic help to near relatives, making a will to pass on property to a chosen heir and demand for support in all social and health crises from the chosen heir and intense interaction with the chosen heir's family.

Pattern of adjustment to a living with family members with independency sustained

An important aspect of the living of the retirees is independence. Many retirees think that if independence is lost they cannot lead comfortable life. So there is a category of adjustment where the retirees live with other family members with this factor sustaining. The perception of this category of retirees is that independent way of life is the one which gives them peace and tranquility. These retirees are keen to avoid economic dependence on children and also they keep away from imposing their own ideals of familial rules and social behaviour on their children.

This pattern of adjustment reveals independence of a retiree in several matters including financial management, decision regarding the transfer of properties, procurement of medical help and conducting of socio-religious functions. These are the characteristic features of a retiree under this pattern of adjustment in spite of the fact that he or she lives with his or her children and participates in important family events and takes part in certain decision-making events too.

Pattern of adjustment to living with other family members with dependency factors associated

Dependency is inevitable to many in old age. As the age increases many conditions drive the retirees to seek the help of their children or other members in the family. This variety of adjustment is a necessary condition for those retirees who cannot exist independently owing to many reasons. Health is one important physical factor reported by the retirees for their dependency on their children, wives or grand-children. As age increases health deteriorates and eventually financial and familial dependency increases. So, the adjustment exists in this manner which is compatible with the physical conditions of the retirees. This pattern of adjustment reveals the increase in the retiree's dependence on his children, wife or grand-children along with age as ill-health is the cause behind the dependence. All important decisions are wrested with wife or eldest son including financial and socio-religious matters in these conditions. So independence in majority of the events is the key feature of this kind of adjustment.

Religious Activities and Socio-psychological Problems 8

According to Orbach, "most people carry on the religious beliefs and habits formed earlier in life" (Orbach 1961: 16,530-540). In old age religious beliefs give a great solace and help to carry on their life forward without much troubles. Covalt has pointed out that ``the attitude of most older people about religion is probably most often that with which they grow up or which they have accepted as they achieved intellectual maturity" (Covalt 1965: 215-224). However, the realization of the place of religion in life is liable to change in the course of life (Soodan 1975: 138-139).

Studies relating to religious practices and beliefs in old age indicated both an intensification of interest and also decline in it. As Havighurst and Albrecht have observed, "There is no evidence of a large-scale turning to religion as they (the people) grow old." (Havighurst and Albrecht 1953). According to the Geriatric Focus Report (Geriatric Focus Report 1966: 5, 9, 4-5) "the thesis that religious faith and practice increase in importance as death approaches which has become part of the folklore of the psychology of religion – now is increasingly challenged by psychologists and social scientists."

This chapter examines the religious activities and problems and socio-psychological problems of the sample respondents. In this regard it highlights the participation of the retirees in prayers, study of religious books and literature, listening to religious discourses and so on, continuity of or change in pre-retirement religious interests, time spent on religious activities, the method of satisfying the religious interest, the persons from whom help is received in the fulfillment of religious interests and utilization of leisure time for several religious and non-religious activities. The discussion shows how majority of the retirees show an increased need for religious experience, how an overwhelming proportion continue their pre-retirement religious interests even after their retirement, how commitment to religion is more serious among a few who spend more time in religious practices, how dependence on children for financial support to fulfil some religious activities create disappointment among the retirees, and how the pursuit of leisure time activity with the help of family members sometimes become hard.

While examining the socio-psychological problems of the retirees, the description not only specifies the problems but also shows the approaches of the retires of those problems. The discussion centers round the problems of social isolation and loneliness, perception on special position given to the retirees as aged persons, lack of companionship due to demise of spouse, friend, child and grand-child, ambitions of the retirees in terms of children's' welfare, religious interest, physical and mental well being, creative and intellectual activities and economic matters, perception on urbanization type of the family, relations with kith and kin, generation gap and management of the family. In this connection it tries to depict why some retirees have grater sophistication than others to socio-psychological issues, how those retirees who are regarded in high esteem feel great about it, how the non-gazetted need more emotional support from the younger members of their family, how lack of companionship create lack of diversion among the retirees, why the non-gazeted have his ambitions for their children to come up well in life, how the differential understanding on urbanization reflects the differential responses to adjustment to modern issues, how ideal family size is adhered to, how relations with children change with the change in age of the respondents and how retirees make adjustments to overcome generation gap.

RELIGIOUS ACTIVITIES OF THE RETIREES

Prayers

Table-43 reveals the percentage distribution of the retirees according to their praying pattern. Not less than 28 percent on average pray daily in the morning, about 31.5 percent pray at the time of going to bed.

Thirty five percent of the retirees offer prayers occasionally, that is, Hindus during festivals, Christians on Sundays and Muslims on Fridays. Only 2 percent of the gazetted and 1 percent of the non-gazetted are not having faith in prayers. There is no significant

Table 43. Percentage Distribution of the Retirees accouding to their Praying Pattern

S.No.	Praying pattern	Number of Gazetted Retirees	Number of Non-gazetted Retirees	Total
1	Praying daily			
	Morning	30	26	56 (28%)
	Afternon	3	5	8 (4%)
	Evening (praying at the time of going to bed)	35	28	63 (31.5%)
2.	Praying occasionally	30	39	70 (35%)
3.	Never pray	2	2	3 (1.5%)
	Total	100	100	200 (100%)

difference between the gazetted and the non-gazetted in the prayer pattern.

Participation in religious activities:

Table–44 shows the percentage distribution of the retirees according to their participation in religious activities. The activity of a majority of the retirees is to study religious books and literature. In this category there is not much difference between the gazetted and the non-gazetted retirees.

From the Table–44 it is clear that a little more than one-third of the retirees spend their time in studying religious books and literature and a little less than one-third are listening to religious discourses. A few participate in spiritual discussions and nearly equal proportion of retirees are listening to devotional songs and other programmes.

According to Barron, "religion's gerontological task is essentially four-fold

1. To help face impending death.
2. To help find and maintain a sense of meaningfulness and significance in life.

Table 44. Percentage Distribution of the Retirees according to their Participation in Religious Activities

S.No.	Religious activity	Number of Gazetted Retirees	Number of Non-gazetted Retirees	Total
1	Study of religious books & literature	37	40	77 (38.5 %)
2.	Listening to religious discourses	32	31	63 (31.5%)
3.	Participation in spiritual discussions	11	19	30 (15%)
4.	Listening to devotional songs, dance and other programmes	18	8	26 (13%)
5.	Not interested in any religious activity	2	2	4 (2%)
	Total	100	100	200 (100%)

Chi-square value = 5.5994 (Not significant)

3. To help accept the inevitable losses of old age.
4. To help discover and utilize the compensatory values that are potential in old age." (Barron, 1961)

Pollak explains the role of religion in the following way

"We might say that every aged person is in a hole, and we might expect that older people would show increased needs for religious experience. The anxiety caused by the thought of approaching death seems to be related to various motives. First of all the desire to live and to continue living is apparent in most individuals regardless of age. Further more, religious teaching concerning punishment and reward after death may have created a considerable amount of anxiety in the minds of many regarding the after life. Finally, there may be concern over the fate of dependents who would be left without support (Pollak, 1954).

Table 45. Percentage Distribution of the Retirees according to the continuity of or Change in their Religious Interest

S.No.	Continuity of or religious interest	Number of Gazetted Retirees	Number of Non-gazetted Retirees	Total
1.	Interest increased	30	40	70 (35%)
2.	Interest decreased	23	12	35 (17.5%)
3.	Interests remained the same	45	46	91 (45.5%)
4.	No interest in religion	2	2	4 (2%)
	Total	100	100	200 (100%)

Chi-square value = 4.8962 (Not significant)

The present enquiry confirms the above statement. A majority of the respondents are involved in one or the other religious activity. However, there is not much difference between the gazetted and the non-gazetted in this regard which is apparent from the table.

Table–45 shows the percentage distribution of the retirees according to the continuity or change in interest in religious practices. Slightly more than one-third of the total respondents have changed their religious interests after their retirement whereas nearly half of the respondents have kept up their pre-retirement religious interests even after retirement.

Age plays an important role in the attitudes of the retirees towards religion. This is true with reference to both the gazetted and the non-gazetted retirees. Those retirees whose interest in religion remained the same are the highest in number. This is due to the fact that this category did not equate their achievements and failures with religious attachments or worship of their Gods. Those retirees whose interest increased in religion have two reasons to mention. One is that they developed interest in religion in later years that is after attaining 55. The other is that they have equated their achievements with religion. More than 17 percent of the retirees have shown decrease in interest in religion which can be attributed to the fact that they developed rationalistic attitude on

Table 46. Percentage Distribution of the Retirees according to the Time spent on their Religious Practices

S.No.	Dependence	Number of Gazetted Retirees	Number of Non-gazetted Retirees	Total
1.	One hour	48	46	94 (47%)
2.	Two hours	30	32	62 (31%)
3.	Three hours	17	15	32 (16%)
4.	Four hours	3	5	8 (4%)
5.	Non interested in religion	2	2	4 (2%)
	Total	100	100	200 (100%)

't' value =6.5320 (Significant at 0.01 level)

seeing that neither they are punished for being non-religious nor rewarded for being religious. Age has got a significant role to play in shaping the attitudes of the aged towards religion.

Table–46 give the percentage distribution of the retirees according to the time spent on their religious practices. Almost half of the respondents spend about an hour a day for religious practices.

There is no significant difference in number between the gazetted and the non-gazetted, in the time-spent for their religious practices. Further, only a few, that is less than one-quarter of the respondents could spare three hours or more a day for religious practices.

Those retirees who could spend only one hour a day are engaged in different activities. Some of them are trying to earn more money their livelihood. Some of them are suffering from ill health and some of them are taking care of their grand-children.

Those retirees who spend more than one hour a day in religious practices are relatively free to pursue their religious practices than the former category. Commitment to religion and God is also more serious among a few in this category.

Table–47 delineates the percentage distribution of the retirees according to the method of satisfying their religious interests.

The figures show that of all the categories those who worship at home are more in number. In old-age mobility is less and whatever may be activity, the aged try to perform or conduct it at home, only one-eighth of the total retirees could go on pilgrimage to places like Banaras, Gaya, Prayag and Rameswaram. This category is the one which can afford the cost and also it is the retiree's life-time wish to go on pilgrimage. Those retirees who can move out freely and go to temple for worshipping are also in good number comprising 31 percent of the total respondents. Regular worship is performed by these retirees in a temple or at some other place of worship. The temples and places of public worship serve not only as religious centres but also as meeting places of friends with similar interest.

Not all retirees visit places of public worship or temples. Some of them cannot go there for reasons of health and physical disabilities. They sit in some corner of the house or pooja room and perform their worship. However, there are two respondents of this

Table 47. Percentage Distribution of the Retirees according to the Method of Satisfying their Religious Interests

S.No.	Method	Number of Gazetted Retirees	Number of Non-gazetted Retirees	Total
1.	By regular worship at home	40	38	78 (39%)
2.	By regular worship at a temple or mosque or church	30	32	62 (31%)
3.	By regular sorship at home as well as temple or mosque or church	13	18	31 (15.5%)
4.	By going on pilgrimage to various places	15	10	25 (12.5%)
5.	Not interested in religion	2	2	4 (2%)
	Total	100	100	200 (100%)

type who are keen on visiting the temples in the town at least on important sacred days. But their children deny to take them from their home to these places. So, this has become a problem to them. The same two respondents are also keenly interested in the study of religious literature like commentaries on scriptures or works of saints and sages. By going through these sacred texts they wish to have spiritual satisfaction. But their children advise them to be satisfied with the study of the sacred books they have already in their possession rather than going through the new ones. They deny to purchase a few sacred books required by their aged parents.

Likewise, these aged respondents ask their children to take them to the nearest holy places of pilgrimage. Their children have not heeded to their words so far. Thus these two aged respondents are not able to pursue their religious interests and satisfy their spiritual interests because their children are not co-operating with them in religious matters.

Table–48 depicts the percentage distribution of the respondents according to the help received in religious activities. It is apparent from the table that a majority of the retirees received help from their wives in religious activities.

As explained above, more than half of the respondents have received help from their wives, which can be attributed to the fact that wives are the members in any family who give assistance to their husbands in old age. It can also be inferred from the above

Table 48. Percentage Distribution of the Respondents according to the Help Received in Religious Activities

S.No.	Helping Member	Number of Gazetted Retirees	Number of Non-gazetted Retirees	Total
1.	Wife	60	48	108 (54%)
2.	Children	23	41	64 (32%)
3.	Friends	15	9	24 (12%)
4.	Not interested	2	2	4 (2%)
	Total	100	100	200 (100%)

table that children and friends pay less attention towards the retirees in carrying the latter's religious activities. Those retirees who are not in a position to receive help from their wives are helped by children and friends. There is not any significant variation between the gazetted and the non-gazetted in this respect.

M. Sudheer Kumar Babu, aged 67 years, is a retiree from Electricity Department. He is helped by his friends in religious activities. He maintains a balance between his religious interests and his daily routine by a careful planning to suit his mode of life. He is in the habit of conducting daily worship in a room of his house and visiting the local temple of Lord Rama in the evenings. He is also interested in the study of sacred books. He has some intimate friends equally interested in the study of religious literature. Visiting them and receiving them at his own residence are normal features of his daily routine. His grown up sons want him to curtail his visits to the temple and to his friends and ask him to conduct worship only in the pooja room of the house. But he argues that his religious interest is a life-long habit which he acquired during his earlier days and intensified after entering service. However, his grown up sons demand that he should not spend on books, that he should not spend on large scale worship and that he should not move in the company of his like-minded friends. But he says that simply because his grown up sons are contributing more income than himself to the family, it does not mean that he must lose interest in his religious activities for the sake of saving a petty sum from the earnings of his sons.

Utilization of leisure–time

Retirees utilized some of their leisure time in the worship of God. More number of the gazetted retirees than the non-gazetted (4:1) spend their time attending clubs and more number of gazetted than non-gazetted (5:3) joined various association in spending time. An equal number of gazetted and non-gazetted retirees spend their leisure time by reading books, magazines, news papers and also going to the market, meeting people and gossiping. More number of non-gazetted than gazetted (2:1) spend part of their leisure time reading religious literature.

Utilization of leisure-time and free-time for recreational activities without financial assistance from youngsters has become a problem for a non-gazetted retiree (N. Mukunda Murthy) and a gazetted retiree (L. Muniswamy Naidu). Ordinarily leisure is understood as the time when man is free from demands of his work. As Lunderberg has pointed out, leisure is the time in which we are free from the more obvious and formal duties which a paid job or other obligatory occupations impose upon us (Lundberg, 1943:33). Free-time is leisure-time in the sense that an individual is not under any constraints to use it in specific ways except according to his own free will.

One gazetted retiree and a non-gazetted retiree experience difficulty in utilizing their free time satisfactorily and enjoy it as leisure-time. The gazetted retiree participated in a popular club and possessed some creative hobbies. He was not able to continue his club activities and pursue his creative hobbies because he was not able to pool resources to meet these needs. His married sons who are well placed have not contributed the money he needed in addition to what he saved every month. One can hardly think of leisure activity that can be enjoyed without pending money: it may be from trifling amounts to much more than can be afforded. Therefore, he had given up his club activities but continue his creative hobbies. The non-gazetted retirees has to face almost similar problem, namely lack of adequate finances to pursue his preferred leisure-time activities.

Both the gazetted retiree and the non-gazetted retiree had their own company to sit with and gossip. Their meetings took place at the homes of their friends. Such meetings served the purpose of an effective form for the exchange of views, experiences and ideas. Many of the day-to-day personal problems were discussed at those meetings. Current political situations were a favorite topic of discussions among them. For the last one and half years, they could not continue their leisure time activities. They could not meet people at their homes as frequently as they would like to, because it required money to get proper clothes and to entertain them when they paid him return visits. Therefore, they were forced to remain confined to their house and spend their time alone. As parents they are too proud to ask their children for money. However, their children who are now drawing good salaries have not come forward to provide them money to spend on their leisure time activities. To these two retired employees, who are experiencing difficulty in utilizing free-time, time has become a burden. They have no free-time activities adequate enough to keep them engaged and busy.

They are trying to depend on their family groups for the pursuit of leisure time activities but they are finding it hard to cultivate those activities within their family groups.

SOCIO-PSYCHOLOGICAL PROBLEMS AND APPROACHES

Social isolation and loneliness

K.S. Soodan says; "Among psychological and environmental factors leading to the emotional living of the aged are a sense of being unwanted, a sense of uselessness, a feeling of loneliness, not necessarily caused by being alone, a feeling of boredom due to the absence of a goal in life, the speed of modern living with the changes in environment placing great stresses and strains on the aged and finally the complexity of demands and natural thought of approaching death. To these may be added their concern for the members of their families, specially those who are yet to stand on their own feet (Soodan,1975).

Social psychologists view individual personality as a `social self', which is influenced by society's or the group's attitudes, tensions, frustrations and its cultural view points. When this 'self' is mentally and emotionally disturbed and becomes physically ill, the causes of the disturbances are to be found in the family, in the neighborhood or society.

Keplan quoted Midleman saying that"aging is more disturbing in a society whose culture provokes irreverence towards the aged, and where economic competition works to their disadvantage." (Kaplan, 1945: 350).

Social and cultural factors weigh heavily in considering the mental health and illness among older persons. The kind of social relations in which the aged engage is a crucial factor in the origin of their mental disorders (Barron, Milton 1961). Psychologists and sociologists have tried to characterize some of these social relations as "loss of significance" (Jung's), "Anomie" (Durkheim's). But relationship between mental disorders and social participation operates in the reverse also. Mental breakdown excludes the patient from social participation. 'Loss of significance' and isolation, or failure to retain a place in the community, or to remain an active member of a family means lack of social integration which is one of the possible causes of the onset of mental disorders.

Table 49. Percentage Distribution of the Retirees according to Social Isolation and Loneliness

S.No.	Response	Number of Gazetted Retirees	Number of Non-gazetted Retirees	Total
1.	Isolated	12	37	49 (24.5%)
2.	Not isolated	88	63	151 (75.5%)
	Total	100	100	200 (100%)

Chi–square value= 16. 8942, (Significant at 1% level)

On critically observing the following issues of socio-psychological interests it can be said that Hypothesis H_6 is true which says that "Gazetted retirees by virtue of their better educational levels have greater sophistication to socio-psychological issues than the non-gazetted retirees."

Table–49 gives the percentage distribution of the retirees according to their social isolation and loneliness. It is interesting to note that three-fourths of the respondents amswered that they are not isolated.

Many gazetted retirees did not feel that they are isolated from others after retirement whereas slightly more than one-third of the non-gazetted felt that they are isolated from others. This is suggestive of financial and psychological independence of the retired non-gazetted employees while it is apparent that more non-gazetted retirees would have liked closer rapport with others.

Table–50 shows the percentage distribution of the retirees according to their perception of isolation.

Among the 12 gazetted retirees who felt that they were isolated, 7 said that they felt isolated from relatives and friends and 5 said that they felt isolated from their family members. Among the 37 non-gazetted retirees, 17 felt that they are isolated from their family and the rest felt that they are isolated from relatives, friends and family members. the feeling of isolation by the retirees may be a feeling of self-defence to account for the decrease in the productivity monetarily or otherwise after retirement. Many other factors like the generation gap, children being employed and busily attending

Table 50. Percentage Distribution of the Retirees according to their Perception of Isolation: "From Whom they are Isolated"

S.No.	Isolated from	Number of Gazetted Retirees	Number of Non-gazetted Retirees	Total
1.	Family	5 (41.66%)	17 (45.95%)	22 (44.89%)
2.	Relatives and friends	7 (58.34%)	14 (37.83%)	21 (42.85%)
3.	Both	—	6 (16.22%)	6 (12.26%)
	Total	12 (100%)	37 (100%)	49 (100%)

Chi-square value= 0.0678

to their work may be the causes for making these people feel isolated.

This proves the hypothesis H_6: Gazetted retirees by virtue of their better educational levels have greater sophistication to socio-psychological issues than the non-gazetted retirees.

Perception on special position given to them as the aged

Table–51 reveals the percentage distribution of the retirees according to their perception of the special position given to them as the aged. More than 48 of the total retirees felt great about they being given a special position as the aged.

Equal number of the gazetted and the non-gazetted retirees fell depressed about the fact that they are treated as the aged. This is purely a psychological approach and also it depends upon the factor as to how the retirees are regarded as aged. If the retirees are regarded in high esteem than they feel great about it.

Table-52 reveals the percentage distribution of the retirees according to the information on remaining with the family members in a complete day.

More non-gazetted than gazetted retirees spent more than 3 hours with their family members, while more gazetted than non-

Table 51. Percentage distribution of the Retirees according to their Perception of the Special Position given to them as the Aged

S.No.	Response	Number of Gazetted Retirees	Number of Non-gazetted Retirees	Total
1.	Feel great about it	43	54	97 (48.5%)
2.	Feel depressed about it	37	36	73 (36.5%)
3.	Feel indifferent to it	20	10	30 (15%)
	Total	100	100	200 (100%)

Chi-square value= 4.5945 (Not Significant)

gazetted retirees spent less than 3 hours with the family members. This again is suggestive of more emotional support needed by the non-gazetted retirees. Spending time with others requires the willingness on both sides: the retiree and his family.

Table 52. Percentage Distribution of the Retirees according to the Information on Remaining with the Family Members in a Complete Day

S.No.	Time spent with family members	Number of Gazetted Retirees	Number of Non-gazetted Retirees	Total
1.	Remain with others for 3 hours or more	33	41	74 (52.11%)
2.	Remain with others for less than 3 hours	35	19	54 (38.03%)
3.	Remain mostly alone	7	7	14 (9.86%)
	Total	75	67	142 (100%)

Chi-square value= 5.6056 (Not significant)

Table 53. Percentage Distribution of the Retirees according to the Information on Indication of Lack of Companionship

S.No.	Indication	Number of Gazetted Retirees	Number of Non-gazetted Retirees	Total
1.	Losing spouse	4	2	6 (11.32%)
2.	Losing friend	15	16	31 (58.49%)
3.	Losing grand-children	2	3	5 (9.44%)
4.	Losing children	5	6	11 (20.75%)
	Total	26	27	53 (100%)

Chi–square value= 0.2770 (Significant at 1% level)

Lack of companionship due to death

Table–53 shows the percentage distribution of the retirees according to the information on indication of lack of companionship. As age advances and the person retirees it is but natural that he would have faced quite a number of sorrowful occasions like losing the spouse, children or grand-children, or friends. As most of the friends of a retired person are near his age, it was found that more people lost their friends than spouse, children or grand-children. A feeling of loneliness due to any death is but natural and it is felt more by the aged persons due to lack of diversion.

The figures in the table reveal that the retirees suffer mostly from lack of companionship on account of losing friends. Majority of the retirees from both the categories have expressed their opinion that they lack companionship due to losing friend. This is because in old age friends of their age give good emotional support. Losing children is also an important cause of lack of companionship. Gazetted and non-gazetted retirees do not show differential patterns in this respect.

Ambitions of the retirees

Table–54 shows the percentage distribution of the retirees according to their ambitions. Child-centred ambitions occupy a place of primacy over other types of ambitions. Next to this is the

Table 54. Percentage Distribution of the retirees according to their Ambitions

S.No.	Ambitions	Number of Gazetted Retirees	Number of Non-gazetted Retirees	Total
1.	Child-centred ambitions	25	37	62 (31%)
2.	Religious and other worldly ambitions	15	20	35 (17.5%)
3.	Ambitions for physical and mental health	37	17	54 (27%)
4.	Creative and intellectual ambitions	10	13	23 (11.5%)
5.	Economic centred ambitions	13	13	26 (13%)
	Total	100	100	200 (100%)

ambition for physical and mental health. This is a consequence of old age.

A majority of the retirees had ambitions centering around their children. In this group there are more non-gazetted retirees than the gazetted retirees. More gazetted than non-gazeted retirees have ambition for physical and mental health. A few have ambition centering around money, intellect and religion. As the non-gazetted would have felt throughout their life that they are subordinates it is quite natural that they have high ambitions for their children to come-up well in life.

Perception on urbanization

Table–55 shows the percentage distribution of the retirees according to their perceptions of the changed conditions in the family which have a direct bearing upon urbanization. More gazetted retirees have agreed with the above statement. By virtue of their position as administrators they inculcate the changes in the society and understand the urbanization effect.

Table 55. Percentage Distribution of the Retirees according to their perception of the Changed conditions in the family which have a Direct bearing upon urbanization

S.No.	Response	Number of Gazetted Retirees	Number of Non-gazetted Retirees	Total
1.	Agree	68	51	119 (39.5%)
2.	Disagree	22	33	55 (27.5%)
3.	Neutral	10	16	26 (13%)
	Total	100	100	200 (100%)

Chi-square value=6.0132 (Significant at 5% level)

Considering the figures in the table, more number of the gazetted had a positive approach while more non-gazetted had a negative or neutral approach towards the fact that urbanization has affected family conditions. By their official status the non-gazeted are more conservative as they do not get exposed to modern issues in the society. But the gazetted officers deal with the issue and encounters in the process of their job in the office. So the gazetted retirees understands and agrees with the fact that the changed conditions have direct bearing upon urbanization.

So the problem is that the aged persons are not healthily in congruence with the changes that are favouring urbanization.

Perception on family type

Table–56 delineates the percentage distribution of the retirees according to their perception of family type. It discusses about the percentage distribution of the respondents according to their perception of the family composition. Significantly high number of gazetted retirees have given their option for the family with parents and two children.

The ratio of gazetted officers who felt that a family should contain parents and two children versus parents and three children was nearly 2:1. While the same ratio in non-gazetted was 1:1. Possibly the awareness of limiting the family to two children in the gazetteed

Table 56. Percentage Distribution of the Retirees according to their Perception of Family–Type

S.No.	Family type	Number of Gazetted Retirees	Number of Non-gazetted Retirees	Total
1.	Parents + 2 Children	67	48	115 (57.5%)
2.	Parents + 3 Children	28	43	71 (33.5%)
3.	Parents + 4 Children and above	5	9	14 (7%)
	Total	100	100	200 (100%)

officers is due to their higher aspirations about their children. It is very heartening to note that both the gazetted and non-gazetted retirees do not want four children or above and only 7% of the total gave a positive answer to this question. Analyzing these cases it was found that a large number of this 7 % had four or more children. It is clear from the table that description that more non-gazetted than gazetted retirees have shown disinterest towards smaller families which in turn creates problems to themselves, that is, the non-gazetted retirees.

Family orientations and kin-group relations

Table-57 delineates the percentage distribution of the respondents according to their perception of family as the basic group for care of the older persons. A nearly equal number of gazetted and non-gazetted retirees believe that the family is the group for the care of the older persons.

From the Table–57 it is clear that those who disagree with the above statement are in equal number in both the gazetted and non-gazetted retirees. So it is as clear as crystal that the inter-personal relations in the families of both the categories of respondents are quite similar. Those retirees who agree with the fact that family is the basic group for the care of the older persons are also nearly in equal number in both the categories. Slightly

Table 57. Percentage Distribution of the Respondents according to their perception of Family as the Basic Group for Care of the Older persons

S.No.	Response	Number of Gazetted Retirees	Number of Non-gazetted Retirees	Total
1.	Agree	63	54	117 (58.5%)
2.	Disagree	27	28	55 (27.5%)
3.	Neutral	10	18	28 (14%)
	Total	100	100	200 (100%)

Chi- square value=2.9962 (Non significant)

more than one-fourth of the total retirees are not clear in this regard and this may be that they could not judge their position in the family against the above statement. In this group there are more number of non-gazetted retirees because of their low level of intellect, which is necessary to ascertain one's position in his family. Nearly one-fourth of the retirees disagree with the fact that family is the basic group for care of the older people and this shows that a significant number of older people are disenchanted with the contemporary familial conditions.

Mr. M. Harish Kumar Reddy, a retired gazetted officer, says" Family is the basic unit for the care of the older persons." He has a good family rapport with his married sons and their wives and look after him affectionately.

Mr. S.M. Adikesavulu naidu, a retired non-gazetted officer, disagrees with the above opinion even though he is properly taken care of by his children. The reason attributed is that the inevitable responsibilities on the aged person stand in way of the fact that family is the basic group for the care of the aged.

Relations with children

Table-58 shows the percentage distribution of the retirees according to their perception that change in relation with children occurs along with age. Although nearly half of them have agreed

Table 58. Percentage Distribution of the Retirees according to their perception on "Change in relations with Children occurs Along with Age'

S.No.	Response	Number of Gazetted Retirees	Number of Non-gazetted Retirees	Total
1.	Agree	54	43	97 (48.5%)
2.	Disagree	30	40	70 (35%)
3.	Neutral	16	17	33 (16.5%)
	Total	100	100	200 (100%)

Chi-square value=2.7063 (Not Significant)

with the above fact, the other half not agreed with the above statement.

Among those who said that there is a change in relation there are more gazetted retirees while among the non-gazetted there is a near equal number of those who agree and disagree with the above statement. It seems that the gazetted retirees expected more from their children which was not fulfilled and hence felt that there is a change in the relationship with their children. Nearly half of the retirees agreed that there is a change in relation with their children along with their age. This is suggestive of the problems due to generation gap and understanding between people of different generations.

Opinion regarding children consulting them on important family matters

Table–59 gives the percentage distribution of the retirees according to their opinion on children consulting them on important family matters. It is obvious from the table that a big number of aged who comprise more than half of the total retirees feel bad if children do not consult them on important family matters. The difference between the gazetted and the non-gazetted is not significant in the above category.

Table 59. Percentage Distributiion of the Retirees according to their Opinion on Children Consulting them on important Family Matters

S.No.	Opinion	Number of Gazetted Retirees	Number of Non-gazetted Retirees	Total
1.	Not necessary for the children to consult	26	19	45 (22.5%)
2.	Feel bad if not consulted	48	57	105 (52.5%)
3.	Feel happy if not bothered to consult	17	7	24 (12%)
4.	No child to consult	9	17	26 (13%)
	Total	100	100	200 (100%)

Chi-square value=8.4885 (Significant at 5% level)

Nearly one eighth of the total employees felt that it is not necessary for children to consult them and that the children could take their own decisions. In this group there were more gazetted retirees than the non-gazetted, but in the group (12%) where the retirees felt they would be happy if left alone and not bothered about family matters, there were more gazetted than non-gazetted. From the above three answers it is apparent that the gazetted officers felt more secure and did not bother about their children taking independent decisions while the non-gazetted employees felt less secure and wanted to have a say in the family matters thereby proving their importance.

Perception on children's approach to traditional values

Table-60 reveals about the percentage distribution of the retirees according to their perception on children's approach to traditional values. Eventhough the number of retirees who said that no deviation from traditional values is permitted is only 41.5 percent, this group is more in number than the other two groups which gave different responses.

From the table it is clear that among those who insisted upon no

Table 60. Percentage Distribution of the Retired According to their perception on Children's Approach to Traditional Values

S.No.	Opinion	Number of Gazetted Retirees	Number of Non-gazetted Retirees	Total
1.	No deviation from traditional values is permitted	37	46	83 (41.5%)
2.	Some deviation is permitted	32	28	60 (30%)
3.	No insistence on traditional values	31	26	57 (28.5%)
	Total	100	100	200 (100%)

Chi-square value=1.6812 (Not significant)

variation from traditional values, there are more non-gazetted than the gazetted retirees. This is suggestive of acceptance of permissiveness in the society by the more educated and well-placed members in this advancing age. There is not much difference between the gazetted and the non-gazetted where the retirees have answered for some permission of deviation from traditional values and methods, which is indicating that education and official status do not always decide perceptions of progressive or retirees have said that they do not insist on traditional values. In this group also there is not much difference between the two categories and by which the above hypothesis is holding good. A good majority of 83 percent of the retirees do not permit their children to deviate from traditional values which is again a problem with the older generation sticking to their guns and not understanding the changes that are taking place among the people of younger generation.

Mr. K.M. Narayana Murthy is a retiree who is traditional and conservative in opinions. He says "I do not permit my children to deviate from traditional values as these values are the guiding principles for children."

Mr. S. Kiran Kumar Reddy who is also a retiree of the same age says "I permit my children to deviate from traditional values as

Table 61. Percentage Distribution of the Retirees according to the Perception on the Best person to Decide children's Interests

S.No.	Best person	Number of Gazetted Retirees	Number of Non-gazetted Retirees	Total
1.	Father - head	31	46	77 (38.5%)
2.	Father, mother and children jointly	59	42	111 (55.5%)
3.	Children themselves	10	12	22 (11%)
	Total	100	100	200 (100%)

things around us have changed along with time."

Best person to decide children's interests

Table-61 shows the percentage distribution of the respondents according to the perception that who is the best person in the family to decide children's interests. The table reveals that more than half of the total retirees have answered that father, mother, and children should jointly decide children's interests.

A majority of the retired employees from both the categories felt that father, mother, and children should jointly decide about the interests of the children suggesting more understanding on the part of the aged. Among those who felt that the father or the head of the family is the best person to decide the children's interest there were more non-gazetted retirees again indicative of the feeling of insecurity in the non-gazetted retiree and his wish to retain a firm grasp on the children.

Mr. A.R. Naidu, a non-gazetted retiree, says' "Father is the best person to decide children's interests as the father is the most experienced male member in a family and in nurturing children. `Experience' is one point which plays a great part in shaping children's future."

Perception on retirees' attitudes to maintain the family

Table–62 shows the percentage distribution of the retirees according to the perception or required attitudes to maintain the

Table 62. Percentage Distribution of the Retirees according to their perception on required Attitudes to Maintain the Family

S.No.	Required attitude	Number of Gazetted Retirees	Number of Non-gazetted Retirees	Total
1.	Authoritarian	30	47	77 (38.5%)
2.	Democratic	70	53	123 (69.5%)
	Total	100	100	200 (100%)

Chi-square value=6.1028 (significant at 1% level)

family. A majority of the retirees, both gazetted and non-gazetted, favoured democratic attitudes.

The table delineates that much more gazetted than the non-gazetted retirees felt that a democratic set-up is required to maintain the family. Authoritarian approach is preferred by more non-gazetted retirees than gazetted retirees. The non-gazetted retirees having served in subordinate services throughout their life do not expect to continue in the same manner but would like to dominate at least their children after retirement.

Authoritarian attitudes and approaches are outmoded and a significant number of the retirees clinging to this way of dealing with things shows nothing but their problematic approach which brings them conflicts in the times to come.

Identification of generation gap

Table–63 shows the percentage distribution of the retirees according to their perception on identifying the generation gap. Many retirees have identified the generation gap by judging the values to which the young are giving preference.

Less than one-fourth of the total employees identified the generation gap by observing the lack of communication while slightly more than one-fourth of the total employees identified the generation gap by observing the lack of mutual understanding between themselves and their children. In this group there are more gazetted retirees who understood the generation gap clearly,

Table 63. Percentage Distribution of the Retirees according to their Perception on Identifying the Generation Gap

S.No.	Identification of generation gap	Number of Gazetted Retirees	Number of Non-gazetted Retirees	Total
1.	By seeing the lack of mutual under-standing	31	26	57 (28.5%)
2.	By seeing the communication	18	19	37 (18.5%)
3.	By judging the values	43	38	81 (40.5%)
4.	By other attitudes	8	17	25 (12.5%)
	Total	100	100	200 (100%)

Chi-square value =4.0143 (Not Significant)

while more non-gazetted than gazetted are not able to define clearly the cause of the generation gap but can only feel about it by the general attitude of the children. The low educational level among the non-gazetted may be the cause for not able to locate the generation gap properly.

Mr. M.L. Rao, a non-gazetted retiree, says; "Identification of generation gap can be made by judging the values and by seeing the communication." He says the above two aspects may be used as tools to identify the generation gap.

Views on younger generation

Table–64 shows the percentage distribution of the retirees according to their perception on younger generation. A clear majority of the retirees have stated that the younger generation are more wise, progressive and independent.

More gazetted retirees felt that the younger generation is more wise, progressive and independent. A near equal number of gazetted retirees and non-gazetted retirees felt that the younger generation is is frustrated and rebellious. A merge difference is found between the gazetted and the non-gazetted who felt that the younger generation thoughtless and has no ideals. The same marginal gap is seen between the gazetted and the non-gazetted when they expressed about the selfish and individualistic nature of the younger

Table 64. Percentage Distribution of the Retirees according to their Perception on Younger Generation

S.No.	Perception of younger generation	Number of Gazetted Retirees	Number Non-gazetted Retirees	Total
1.	More wise, progressive and independent	41	30	71 (35.5%)
2.	Frustrated and rebellious	19	20	39 (19.5%)
3.	Not possessing ideals and thoughts	18	28	46 (23%)
4.	Fashionable and expensive habits	20	17	37 (18.5%)
5.	Individualistic and selfish	2	5	7 (3.5%)
	Total	100	100	200 (100%)

generation. From all these details and from the quantitative data given in the table it can be understood that more number of no-gazetted retirees are discontent with the younger generation probably due to their own inflexible attitude.

Opinion on children's education

Table–65 shows the percentage distribution of the retirees according to their opinion on children's education. It is clear from the table that there is a mixed response from the respondents when asked about their children's career.

More number of gazetted retirees expressed their opinion that their children should study what they plan for them or as per their aptitude. On the contrary many non-gazetted retirees have decided that their children should study either what they dictate to them or as per the availability of seats in the colleges. Here the problem is with many non-gazetted retirees who do not know how to shape their children's career. So the non-gazetted retirees due to their lesser exposure to educational matters, cannot guide their children's lives as do the gazetted retires.

Table 65. Percentage Distribution of the Retirees according to their Opinion on Children's Education

S.No.	Opinion	Number of Gazetted Retirees	Number Non-gazetted Retirees	Total
1.	I want my son/ daughter to choose any course of study they like	36	41	77 (38.5%)
2.	I will determine which course my son/daughter should study	44	19	63 (31.5%)
3.	Childless retirees	7	8	15 (7.5%)
	Total	100	100	200 (100%)

Opinion on children's marriages

Table–66 shows the percentage distribution of the retirees according to their opinion on children's marriages. Most of the retirees opine that arranged marriages are better and the brides or grooms must be from outside the family circle.

The Table–66 clearly shows that a good majority of the gazetted retirees have a rational approach to their children's marriage. The non-gazetted retirees approach to marriage is a bit conservative and unsophisticated as revealed by the responses obtained. As arranged marriages are common in our society there is not much of a difference in this aspect between the gazetted and non-gazetted categories.

The preceding two tables on children's education and marriage prove the hypotheses given below:

H_6 : Gazetted retirees by virtue of their better educational levels have greater sophistication to socio-psychological issues than the non-gazetted retirees.

H_7 : There is a considerable gap in the attitudinal approach of the gazetted and non-gazetted retirees to different issues which include children's education and marriage.

Table 66. Percentage Distribution of the retirees according to their Attidue on Children's Marriage

S.No.	Attitude	Number of Gazetted Retirees	Number of Non-gazetted Retirees	Total
1.	Arranged marriages are better	36	34	70 (35%)
2.	I prefer matches from outside our family circle	43	21	64 (32%)
3.	I prefer matches for my children among our family relatives (consanguineal marriages)	14	37	51 (25.5%)
4.	Childless retirees	7	8	15 (7.5%)
	Total	100	100	200 (100%)

These two hypotheses explain about the refined and progressive approach of the gazetted retirees as against the conservative approach of the non-gazetted retirees.

Health Conditions and Problems

9

Phelps and Handerson described "Old age is a natural and normal condition ------------------ that its pathologies are the same as those that occur at any other age period, but they are intensified by illness, family disorganization, unemployability, reduced income and dependency." (Phelps and Handerson 1952: 217). Of all the problems of old age, the problem of health is a major unsolved problem because it is accentuated by an "increasing number of physical handicaps, more frequent and serious illnesses, more mental disturbances and a general reaction among the aged that ill health is their major burden" (Ibid :225).

According to Goldfarb "a common emotionally determined view of old age is that it is a period of illness, weakness, disability and helplessness about which little or nothing can be done" (Goldfarb:1969).

According to Steiglitz, "Health is that state of being in which all the resume capacities of the organism are at their maximum (Stieglitz, 1950:50). He considers thus an ideal state, an abstraction, unattainable in its perfection, but yet approachable. According to him, there are no specific diseases of old age. "Any illness may occur at any age. But certain disorders increase in frequency after the peak of maturity. These disorders, while not limited to senescents, are nevertheless characteristically geriatric." (Ibid :1950:51).

According to Phelps and Handerson "In addition to the risky economic status of aged the chief causes of dependency are the chronic and degenerative diseases and the physical defects." (Phelps and Handerson 1952:225).

This chapter depicts the health conditions of the subjects of the present enquiry before and after their retirement. While describing the health conditions of the respondents before their retirement attention is drawn to the specific illnesses gone through before retirement and the capacity of the respondents to bear the medical expenses. The data reveals the major health problems of the gazetted and non-gazetted employees and the patterns of similarities and differences in meeting the medical expenses and the financial facilities and constraints involved.

While examining the post-retirement health conditions of the respondents, this chapter deals with the effect of retirement on illness, health status of the retirees, difficulties faced by the retirees in specific activities, financial capacity to meet medical expenses , mental problems, specific addictions such as drinking , smoking and betel-leaf chewing , reasons attributed to such addiction and person who took care of the retirees during their illness.

HEALTH CONDITIONS BEFORE RETIREMENT

Illness gone through just before retirement

The major health problems of the respondent just before the retirement were cataract (20%), back-ache (28%) and arthritis (18%). Many respondents with arthritis also had back-ache, heart–disease blood–pressure and diabetes. These diseases co-existed in 5% to 10% of the patients. Vague non-specific complaints like neuralgia, constipation and avitaminosis were complained by a few. A little more than 10% complained of general weakness.

Table 67. Percentage Distribution of the Retirees according to the Illness gone through just before Retirement

S.No.	Illness	Number of Gazetted Retirees	Number Non-gazetted Retirees	Total
1.	Cataract	16	24	40 (20%)
2.	Back-ache	32	24	56 (28%)
3.	Arthritis	21	15	36 (18%)
4.	Multiple Complaints	1	8	18 (9%)
5.	Those without any complaint	20	29	49 (24.5%)
	Total	100	100	200 (100%)

Diabetes, cataract, heart-disease, blood pressure and arthritis are all diseases that increase in frequency with age. Bronchitis occurring in old age is usually seen in chronic smokers and a few who could not specifically complain of any diseases but were going to the doctors with miscellaneous complaints. These patients were prescribed B-complex tables or capsules and they were included in the avitaminosis group.

Table–67 shows the percentage distribution of the retirees according to their illness gone through by them just before retirement.

The figures in the table show that a majority of the retirees have gone through a number of illnesses just before retirement. There is not much of difference in this respect between the gazetted and the non-gazetted as the diseases mentioned in the table are naturally associated with age.

Capacity to bear medical expenses

Table–68 shows the percentage distribution of the retirees with reference to their capacity to bear medical expenses just before retirement.

It is clear from the above table that a majority of the retirees, that is, more than three-fourths of the total retirees were able to bear their medical expenses. In this, again there were more number of gazetted retirees. Medical expenditure could be borne by financially well off people like the gazetted officers. At the same time nearly one-fourth of the total retirees were not bale to bear the medical expenses owing to financial problems which naturally

Table 68. Percentage Distribution of the Respondents according to their capapcity to bear Medical Expenses before Retiremnt

S.No.	Capacity	Number of Gazetted Retirees	Number of Non-gazetted Retirees	Total
1.	Able to bear	87	69	156 (78%)
2.	Not able to bear	13	31	44 (22%)
	Total	100	100	200 (100%)

exist when a person is at the verge of retirement. That is why even a very small proportion of the gazetted retirees along with only one-third of the non-gazetted retirees are seen in the category of the aged who could not bear medical expenses.

HEALTH CONDITIONS AFTER RETIREMENT

Health status of the retirees

Table–69 shows the percentage distribution of the retirees according to their own assessment of their health status. From the table it is very clear that nearly three-fourths of the retirees felt that they are having good or average health. Twice as many non-gazetted as gazetted retirees felt that their health is bad or worse.

The above table reveals that more non-gazetted retirees fell in the categories of average, bad and worse health conditions. On the other hand, more number of gazetted have reported good health. Economic factor is an important element in the well-being of any person more so in the case of the aged. So, it is because of the above reason that more gazetted than the non-gazetted retirees have reported good health and more non-gazetted than the gazetted retirees have reported average, bad and worse health conditions. Health care of the aged has to go through many processes like routine medical check-up, regular medicines and necessary laboratory investigations.

Table 69. Percentage Distribution of the Retirees according to their Self-assessed Health Status

S.No.	Status of health	Number of Gazetted Retirees	Number Non-gazetted Retirees	Total
1.	Good	47	36	83 (41.5%)
2.	Average	30	33	63 (31.5%)
3.	Bad	12	21	33 (16.5%)
4.	Worse	6	15	21 (10.5%)
	Total	100	100	200 (100%)

Chi-square value= 7.9124 (significant at 5% level)

People become more and more vulnerable to chronic ailments and disabilities as they reach old age. It is a general phenomenon that the ailments and diseases of the aged are multiple and chronic in nature. It is apparent from the table to justify the above statement that a majority of the retirees from both the categories are having various health problems.

Mr. R. Girish Kumar, a retired gazetted officer, observes health precautions by maintaining diet and regular exercise. He says, "Not that I am absolutely free from illnesses but the diet control and regular exercises keep me comfortable in spite of a chronic health disorder."

The above observation is significant in the sense that it speaks about a person maintaining comfortable health condition in spite of a chronic ailment.

Difficulties faced in specific activities

Table–70 shows the percentage distribution of the respondents according to their difficulties in certain specific activities. A majority of the retirees have reported that they find it difficult to do manual work. In this category the difference between the gazetted and the non-gazetted retirees is marginal.

There is a near uniform pattern in the retirees regarding the difficulties faced in specific physical activities. The percentage

Table 70. Percentage Distribution of the Respondents according to the Difficulties faced by them in certain Specific Activities

S.No.	Specific activity	Number of Gazetted Retirees	Number of Non-gazetted Retirees	Total
1.	Climbing stairs	10	8	18 (9%)
2.	Doing manual work	37	40	77 (38.5%)
3.	Walking	20	20	40 (20%)
4.	Daily activities	33	32	65 (32.5%)
	Total	100	100	200 (100%)

Chi-square valaue=0.3545(Not Significant)

distribution with reference to climbing the stairs, walking, routine activities and manual work are in the ascending order of frequency. Since this particular question relates to complete physical fact and does not depend much on socio-economic status or other considerations there is no difference between the gazetted and the non-gazetted categories of retirees.

Among the retirees who reported that they find it difficult to walk at least half a kilometer, nearly half of them are chronic arthritics. Those who said that they find it difficult to climb stairs include both arthritics, asthmatics and patients of again pectoris. So, it is apparent that ill-health restricts physical activities of the aged.

Mr. N. Appa Rao, a retired gazetted officer, says that he faces difficulty in climbing stairs as he is an osteo arthritic. As arthritis is a chronic ailment there is no permanent cure to it. So, Mr. Appa Rao takes Brufen-400 mg strength twice daily and manages to get along with the above ailment.

Table–71 demonstrates the percentage distribution of the retirees according to the frequency of medical treatment required. It is clear from the table that slightly more than one-third of the retirees require occasional medical attention.

The above table delineates that no treatment was required in one-fourth of the retirees. When asked why they did not require

Table 71. Percentage Distribution of the Retirees according to the Frequency of Medical Treatment Required

S.No.	Frequency of medical treatment	Number of Gazetted Retirees	Number of Non-gazetted Retirees	Total
1.	Occasionally	41	38	79 (39.5%)
2.	Regularly	13	17	30 (15%)
3.	Cannot afford	18	23	41 (20.5%)
4.	No treatment required	28	22	50 (25%)
	Total	100	100	200 (100%)

Chi-square value=1.9770 (Not Significant)

any treatment many in this group said that throughout their life they did not have any major health problem and after retirement with less activity and more rest they are much more fit. About 15 percent had a regular medical check-up. This group included those suffering from diabetes, hypertension, coronary artery disease, is chemic heart disease and arthritis. One-fifth of the retirees felt that they could not afford proper medical attention of a specialist owing to economic reasons.

Mr. S. Rama Muni Reddy, a retired non-gazetted employee, says "I require treatment but cannot afford the cost of consultation and medicines. As I am a diabetic and cardiac patient I need frequent medical attention and costly medicines which are out of my reach. So, I am consulting a general practitioner (family doctor). But I am still not completely cured."

The ability to get proper medical attention when ill has made the gazetted retirees feel that their health problems are minimal. Conversely, the lower income non-gazetted retirees tend to exaggerate their medical problems because they could not go for a proper care.

Capacity to bear medical expenses

Table–72 shows the percentage distribution of the retirees according to their capacity to bear medical expenses. The capacity to bear medical expenses has got direct link to one's economic status.

Even though 25 percent of the retirees required no treatment according to the preceding table, they have expressed their concern

Table 72. Percentage Distribution of the Retirees according to their Capacity to Bear medical Expenses

S.No.	Response	Number of Gazetted Retirees	Number of Non-gazetted Retirees	Total
1.	Able to bear	78	56	134 (67%)
2.	Not able to bear	22	44	66 (33%)
	Total	100	100	200 (100%)

Chi-square value=6.0132 (significant at 5% level)

Table 73. Percentage Distribution of the Retirees according to their Mental Problems

S.No.	Mental problems	Number of Gazetted Retirees	Number of Non-gazetted Retirees	Total
1.	Feeling loneliness	20	31	51 (25.5%)
2.	Forgetfulness	6	13	19 (9.5%)
3.	Confusion	18	20	38 (19%)
4.	Lack of interest and initiative	45	26	71 (35.5%)
5.	Reduced mental alertness	11	10	21 (10.5%)
	Total	100	100	200 (100%)

Chi-square value=6.0132 (significant at 5% level)

over soaring medical expenditure in general. Two-thirds of the retirees of whom there were gazetted than non-gazetted felt that they could bear the medical expenses. The medical expenditure constitutes a considerably significant part of a person's income. So it is found that there were more gazetted and less non-gazetted who could bear these expenses.

Mental problems of the retirees

Table–73 shows the percentage distribution of the retirees according to their mental problems. Slightly more than one-third of the total retirees have expressed that they are lacking interest and initiative in any sort of activity.

The figures in the table reveal that only one-tenth of the respondents have the problem of reduced mental alertness. One-fourth of the retirees said that they felt lonely after retirement. These people could not give up the feeling of loss of office and friendship and could not develop new forgetfulness and confusion and these people were mostly above 65 years. On the whole there was not much of a difference found between gazetted and non-gazetted in the mental problems faced.

Mr. Rama Murthy Sarma. a retired gazetted officer from revenue

Service, says "I face the problem of forgetfulness so often that I do not remember even the events that took place yesterday. When I approached doctors they assured me that it is a natural aging process and no treatment is required or possible."

Effect of retirement on illness

Table–74 shows the percentage distribution of the respondents according to the post-retirement effects on their illness. A good number of retirees have said that their illnesses are controlled to some extent. Less than a quarter of them are tolerating these illnesses as before.

The table shows that there are more gazetted who are comfortable with their health after retirement. Five times more than the gazetted are the non-gazetted who said that the post-retirement effect has deteriorated their health. Maintaining health is a financial affair these days and more so in the case of the aged as that the illnesses are troubling them as before are nearly equal in number in both the categories of retirees.

Table 74. Percentage Distribution of the Retirees according to the Post-retirement Effect of Illnesses

S.No.	Post-retirement effect	Number of Gazetted Retirees	Number of Non-gazetted Retirees	Total
1.	They are controlled to some extent	16	10	26 (38.82%)
2.	They are tolearable to me as before	2	8	10 (14.92%)
3.	They are troubling me as before	5	6	11 (16.41%)
4.	They deteriorated my health	3	17	20 (29.85%)
	Total	26	41	67 (100%)

Chi-square value=22.0693 (Significant at 1% level)

Table 75. Frequency Distribution to the Retired according to their Habits and Addictions

S.No.	Habits	Number of Gazetted Retirees			Number of Non-gazetted Retirees			Total
		Regu-larly	Occasi onally	Total	Regu-larly	Occasi onally	Total	
1.	Drinking (Alcoholism)	3	10	13	6	25	31	44
2.	Smoking	40	20	60	50	22	72	132
3.	Chewing of betel leaves and nuts	24	40	64	35	30	65	129
	Total	67	70	137	91	77	168	305

Chi-square values:

Gazetted

Chi-Square value = 14.5268
(Significant at 1% level)

Non-gazetted

Chi-Square value = 21.9287
(Significant at 1% level)

Total : (Gazetted and non-gazetted)

Chi-Square value = 67.8672
(Significant at 1% level)

Addictions of the retirees

Table-75 shows the distribution of the retirees according to their habits and addictions. It is quite evident from the table that a good number of retirees have given a clear picture of their respective addictions.

There are more number of non-gazetted retirees who got addicted to drinking. Many retirees were occasional drinkers. The occasional drinkers among the gazetted and non-gazetted are in the ratio of 2 : 5 and the regular drinkers are in the ratio of 1 : 2. Regular smokers in the gazetted and the non-gazetted are in the ratio of 4: 5 and occasional smokers are in the ratio of 1 : 1. Chewing

Table 76. Frequency Distribution of the Respondents according to the Reasons attributed to Drinking, Smoking and Betel Leaf Chewing

S.No.	Response	Number of Gazetted Retirees	Number of Non-gazetted Retirees	Total
I.	DRINKING			
	i. Helps me to overcome anxiety	2	4	6
	ii. Helps me to control my ailment	4	10	14
	iii. Helps me to keep me warm	2	5	7
	iv. It is my habit, I cannot forget it	5	12	17
	Chi-Square value = 0.0044 (Not Significant)			
II.	SMOKING			
	i. Helps me to work	35	45	80
	ii. Helps me to relieve from asthmatic trouble	10	7	17
	iii. Helps me in bowel movement	20	10	30
	iv. It is my habit, I cannot forget it	5	10	15
III.	BETEL LEAF-CHEWING			
	i. Helps me in my digestion	50	50	100
	ii. Helps me from teeth troubles	5	35	40
	iii. I cannot forget it	9	5	14
	Chi-Square value = 19.7751 (Significant at 1% level)			
	Total	64	90	154

of betel nut and betel leaves was predominant in equal proportions in both the categories of retirees.

The numerical disparity with reference to gazetted and non-gazetted retirees among the occasional drinkers is due to the fact that drinking is a very common feature among Class IV employees who are included in the non-gazetted category. The same is true with regard to regular drinkers who are in the ratio of 1 : 2 among the gazetted and non-gazetted retirees.

Reasons attributed to drinking, smoking and betel leaf chewing

Table–76 shows the frequency distribution of the respondents according to the reasons attributed to drinking, smoking and betel leaf chewing.

Asked about what makes them drink, a good number of them said that they got accustomed to it while working and could not give it up. Some of them said that they are sick and taking alcohol only will keep the disease under control. A few said that it keeps them warm or helps them to overcome anxiety. Whatever reason they are giving, it looks as though they could not give up the habit and are inventing justifiable reasons for continuation of their habits.

Mr. I. Laxmana Murthy, a retired gazetted officer from judicial service, says, "I am addicted to drinking just before retirement as a

Table 77. Percentage Distribution of the Retirees according to the Care taken after them during Illness

S.No.	Person taking care	Number of Gazetted Retirees	Number Non-gazetted Retirees	Total
1.	Wife /husband	40	42	82 (41%)
2.	Sons	33	30	63 (31.5%)
3.	Daughters	5	7	12 (6%)
4.	Daughter-in-law	20	18	38 (19%)
5.	Servants or others	2	3	5 (2.5%)
	Total	100	100	200 (100%)

bid to get rid of certain rare problems." He says, "I can't explain exactly what the problem is as it is very complex and vague."

It is observed that a sort of phobia developed in the mind of Mr. Laxmana Murthy, which resulted in drinking.

A majority of the smokers are accustomed to smoking as part of their office duties. They said that smoking helps them to carry on the office work. A few got so much addicted to it that they have bowel movement only when they smoke. A few accepted the reality that they are addicted and cannot give it up.

A very high percentage of both the gazetted and non-gazetted categories of retirees are betel-leaf chewers. This habit is particularly prevalent in Tirupati which is adjoining Tamil Nadu where this habit is rampant. Half of the betel-leaf chewers say that it helps them in the digestion of their food, one-fourth to one-third say that helps them in curing their teeth trouble and the rest says that they are simply addicted to it.

Persons who take care of the retirees during their illness

Table–77 shows the percentage distribution of the retirees according to the people who take care of the retirees during their illness. A majority of the retirees said that they are taken care of by their wives or husbands.

Wife or husband, if surviving and healthy, is the most logical person to look after the aged person during illness and this was so in slightly less than a quarter of the retirees. Where the wife is ill or dead, sons are looking after the retires and where the sons are busy with their jobs the daughters-in-law are looking after their in-laws suffering from illness.

Custom in India is that the parents usually are looked after by the sons or daughters-in-law and hence the daughters formed only 6 percent who were looking after the aged retirees.

A small group (2.5%) of the retired employees are being looked after by servants, and relatives like brothers and cousins. There was no significant difference in all the above context between the gazetted and non-gazetted retirees.

Summary and Conclusions 10

The universe of this study is a section of the aged population living within the municipal limits of Tirupati, a famous pilgrim town located in the State of Andhra Pradesh in India. The aged population includes employees who retired in the last ten to fifteen years. From this universe of the aged population, 100 gazetted and 100 non-gazetted retirees are selected for the present study. The sample of subjects chosen for the present enquiry represents various ethnic groups, age-groups and work groups among the gazetted and non-gazetted retirees.

By traditional anthropological techniques of interview, schedule, case study and observation, the data was collected between 1987 and 1988. Analysis and presentation of the data are based on simple statistical methods supported by a good number of relevant case studies. The data are presented in simple tables. Arithmetic mean, standard normal probability test and Chi-Square test are used to know the significant differences between the two large sample means and to understand the degree of independence of two attributes respectively.

First, the analysis focused its attention on the working-man complex, demographic features, living conditions, and kin-group orientations besides status as well as influence structure and inter-personal relations within the family group in order to depict the socio-economic conditions of the retirees.

Secondly, the analysis dealt with the opinions of the subjects on traditional values and children, children's marriages, women's education and employment, dowry system, ideal family size, preferred offspring, ideal age at marriage of children, small family norm and family planning and age at retirement in order to know the attitudes of retirees in terms of certain aspects of modernity.

Thirdly, the analysis considered the problems of health in terms of chronic diseases, physical disabilities and mental incapacities in old age, the economic problems in terms of abrupt fall in income, need for more income, lack of savings, effort to save money, using of resources, control over savings and property and taking up an occupation, and the psycho-social problems in terms of social participation and isolation, religious an spiritual interests, leisure and free-time activities and various ambitions in life.

The study reveals that the dynamics of the process of work and retirement are inextricably interwoven with each other. The traditional concept of work is no more valid in the context of modern technology, urbanization and innovation of a number of occupations. Industrialization resulted into a position that the nature of work had to change drastically. Earlier understanding and functions of work have undergone changes as more number of work places and varieties of work have started coming up to meet the modern needs of society.

The results of the study show that the working man complex has played an important role in the lives of the retirees. Working places have provided opportunities for employees to improve their contacts with people from different walks of life. The employees in the work place developed a sense of solidarity towards one another, being very conscious and cautious of the next man's position in the offices and his promotional chances. As the employees acquired this sort of an approach at places of work, retirement from work deprived them from such a milieu where they were enjoying a number of privileges. In this connection it is appropriate to quote Broomley's observations with reference to retirees in U.S.A. He said, "The retirees problem is to find satisfactory ways of disengaging from employment without suffering from economic hardships or emotional deprivations such as loneliness and boredom." (Bromely 1966 : 73).

The study further reveals that planning for retirement and old age is the concern of the gazetted and non-gazetted retirees. They feel concerned about the prospects of the retired life only when it is too late to take any preparatory steps for the problems and contingencies that normally accompany retirement. Recent studies also illuminate similar findings (Bhatia 1983: 48-5-0).

Results of the present inquiry reveal the hierarchical position of specific problems in the life of the retired persons. Problems are found to cluster around pension, family life, proximity of friends, anxiety and insecurity. However, for the gazetted retirees finance and personality are not greater problems than family life and health but for the non-gazetted retirees finance, health and fear of insecurity are greater problems than family life. The problem of housing and its related issues are of greater concern to the non-gazetted than the gazetted. All the gazetted as against none among the non-gazetted fell that retirement brought with it loss of status. Researches on the aged populations in other urban centers in other countries also support these findings (Maddox 1996: 118). The adverse effects of reduced income and economic security are equally associated with many personal and social problems, specially the loss in status, meaningful social relations and exposure to other limitations of an undesirable nature from the point of view of the retirees. Therefore retirement is a social as well an economic event.

Loss of income as a post-retirement deprivation is seen as a major factor among the non-gazetted retirees whereas it is not so high among the gazetted retirees.

The non-gazetted retirees are twice as many as the gazetted retirees who feel that the two activities that effect their finances are social functions and religious ceremonies. This is due to the differential perceptions of the gazetted and non-gazetted retiree about social functions and ceremonies.

Social isolation because of non-involvement in the other than routine activities is characteristic of more number of the non-gazetted retirees The indication is that all the gazetted retirees with a high level of education and relatively high socio-economic status and a few non-gazetted retirees with high socio-economic status have rather internal and external resources so that regardless of age and retirement, highly uniform social participation patterns and interests prevail. This finding supports the conclusions of previous researches (Geist 1968: 53, Strauss, Aldrich & Lipman 1976).

The gazetted and non-gazetted employees are conscious of their economic problems and family and social obligations. For a majority of the non-gazetted employees problems remain with them even after their retirement. A vast majority of both the gazetted and non-gazetted retirees feel that they find it difficult to adjust with the younger generations or they may not command much respect from them after retirement.

Property distribution is one important area where one-third of the gazetted and non-gazetted retirees expressed that they want to keep the property with themselves as long as they are alive. A feeling of insecurity is the reason for these retirees not to handover their properties to their children.

It is significant to note that an overwhelming proportion of the gazetted and non-gazetted retirees run their financial affairs and manage the house either alone or long with their wives. This once again reinforces the fact that there is a sense of insecure feeling among both the gazetted and non-gazetted retirees. The respondents expressed the fear that if they relinquish their responsibilities and hand over them to their children, the former will not be cared after, and ultimately their status in the family will be lost.

Irrespective of their gazetted and non-gazetted status, a good majority of the retirees feel that there is a lot of change in their relationship with their children. Social traditions are compelling the retirees to carry their separate identity into their daily routine, but the youth call them to cope with the changing values and with the new styles of living and aggressive challenges of the outside world to establish their authority in the society. Despite social and economic changes and the consequent emergence of individualistic and secular trends in different aspects of urban life, the family continues to remain the center of life's interests and activities of the non-gazetted as well as the gazetted retirees. The dynamics of adjustment with regard to families conditions before and after retirement of the respondents show almost similar patterns. Predominance of nuclear family can be maintained with less number of difficulties and it also shows the emerging trends in family structure in general. These findings support the observations made by other researches (Goldfrab 1965:16, Blanker 1969, Treas 1975:92).

Both the gazetted and non-gazetted retirees feel that they shall not only be responsible for bringing up their children but also be responsible for making every effort to see that the children settle in their life. Disabled children, widowed daughters and their children, and in exceptional circumstances even adult sons, their wives and children who have no self-support are depending upon their parents. It may not be out of place here to mention that the problem of supporting the children in old age is related to the values of the middle class family in India. Adult sons in India are also expected to support their old parents even when they have themselves gone old enough to need help from their own children. These findings are broadly. In conformity with the theoretical position held in the study that the value orientations of the retirees of their class have had their effect on the family for keeping up the interests of the family members together. This find conforms to the observation made by previous research (Blanker 1969, Bhatia 1983:124).

The results show that the differences in the social, economic, and health problems in a small proportion of the gazetted retirees and non-gazetted retirees are not issues based on the dichotomy of gazetted and non-gazetted status. This conceptualization permits a comprehensive approach to a condition that far transcends official status discriminations. Official status based occupation is the definitional means by which inequality is imposed in the self-concept, activity level, social interaction, economic status and attitudes. But there are certain other statuses such as those based on wealth, activity level and religious experiences which have played a great role in matters of adjustment at some of the gazetted and non-gazetted retirees. A rich non-gazetted retiree is more secure than a poor or middle class non-gazetted retiree. Likewise the security of a wealthy gazetted retiree is greater than that of a gazetted retiree whose income is relatively far less. That means post-retirement adjustment is not always homogeneous.

There has been a considerable demand during the last few years from both the gazetted and non-gazetted retirees for an upward revision of their pension whenever the cost of living index has increased. The pensioners belong to a fixed income group wherein they have too adjust to a truncated income. The pension even after revision, does not keep pace with the price rise. Among the non-gazetted retirees those who have no other source of income than pension are the worse affected in this regard. Unless there is a system of either controlling the prices or increasing the pension to keep in line with the price rise, the economic viability of a pensioner is in a precarious position.

In the absence of any positive social action to ameliorate the economic hardships of the retirees or the aged in general, the financial crisis of the retirees would deepen further. Issues relating to the social role, health care, economic sustenance, leisure utilization and place in the family of the retirees are crucially important. Every effort may be made to formulate an appropriate national policy for the aged people in general and the retired gazetted and non-gazetted employees in particular in India.

On the basis of the results and discussion pertaining to the present investigation, certain significant conclusions with reference to the socio-economic, familial, health and socio-psychological conditions, problems and adjustment can be drawn. The problems of the retirees reveal the intensity of the physical problems and the greater freedom from the socio-psychological problems among the respondents.

The average work life period of a worker or an employee is 35 years. This is stipulated as a standard work life period after considering the work conditions existing in different parts of the country. Different regions have different environmental and ecological conditions to which a particular institute of work conditions itself.

Sometimes political conditions are either reducing or enhancing the work life period of an employee. When the reigns of power were taken by the Telugu Desam Party from the Congress party in the year 1983, the former reduced the retirement age of the Government employee to 55 years. Again due to some political upheavals, and the Supreme Court judgement on Andhra Pradesh Government's Retirement Order, the retirement age of the Government employees was enhanced to 58 years in the year 1985. Because of this confused state, some employees had to retire at 55 years and some had to get reinstatement and retire at 58 years.

Nearly one-fourth of the total number of retirees were less satisfied with life and took immediate retirement. The predominance of non-professional employees shows the fact that a majority of the sample respondents have come from administrative institutions rather than non-administrative institutions.

Retirement begins not exactly on the date of retirement for an older person. On the contrary, it gives in a phased manner when an atmosphere starts building up at the work place which has connotation of retirement. This, on a broad scale, conforms to the point of Atchley who says that person's route to retirement has a significant bearing on what life is like immediately after retirement (Atchley 1982 :120).

Among the retirees, families including members of one and two generations on one side and those of three generations on the other side stand in equal numbers. The two–generation families among the non-gazetted retirees are more than one and half times of those among the gazetted retirees. The reason is that more number of the non-gazetted retirees prefer to live with their married children for security purposes. When the retirees live with their married children it is but natural that the grand-children come into picture.

At the time of retirement the picture is more or less the same but for the sub-types of families and composition. Almost three-fourths of the respondents live in nuclear families either before or after their retirement. However, it may be pointed out that several respondents lived in incomplete and complete nuclear families with dependents before their retirement. Now, few of the retirees live in such types of families because some of the dependents who were ripe in years passed away, some who were sisters, sisters-in-law, brothers-in-law and other near relatives who either moved to their husband's families after marriage or moved to their natal families and some who were physically disabilitated or two were not maintaining good health right from their childhood died.

Before their retirement three spinsters and a married man were living alone but after retirement two widowers and a widow in addition to the three spinsters and a married man, are living alone. Pre and post-retirement figures relating to the types of families thus show an increase in the number of single-member households among the retirees. The vertically extended families are found to be more common than the horizontally extended families among the respondents either before or after retirement.

A significant number of the retirees from both the gazetted and non-gazetted categories feel that there is an abrupt fall in their income. This is probably due to constant spurts in the price index. The contradiction exists in away that the pensions, are not revised on par with the rising price index. After retirement a person is faced with the basic problem of economic needs.

The sources of income are different for different retirees. Nearly half of the retirees from both the gazetted and non-gazetted categories depend upon the pension amount. But the other half supplement their income by other source like business, agriculture, house-rent and post-retirement employment. The retirees have felt that it is their right to seek assistance from sons and the sons felt it their duty to comply with the demand. The custom in Indian families dictates that the daughters should always take things from their parents but should not give things to their parents. More than three-fourths of the gazetted and the non-gazetted retirees have agreed that they run their financial affairs alone and manage the house or jointly control their financial position along with their wives.

The retirees show three distinct patterns of economic adjustment: the well adjusted, the poorly adjusted and the marginally adjusted. The well adjusted are those whose economic life is very less disturbed or who rarely see financial crisis in their life. The poorly adjusted are those who have reduced their economic needs to meet the ongoing expenditure. The marginally adjusted are those retirees who are balancing their financial needs and sources. These patterns of adjustment are in conformity with those adopted by the retirees living in other parts of India (Bhatia 1983:76).

There is a numerical predominance of nuclear families over the other types of families among both the gazetted and non-gazetted retirees. Nuclear and extended families comprise a little less than three-fourth and one-fourth respectively of the total number of families.

The changes in the family structure have occurred owing to different types of situations they had to face before and after retirement of the respondents. There is a direct link between the economic processes, socio-cultural activities and family conditions. This has resulted in the dynamic situations of these families. In spite of these changes family remained the center of a retiree's life and it is following the cyclic course from one structure to another and has proved that it is not breaking up as predicted by certain utopion theories relating structural changes among families. The family is bending, adjusting or adapting to the changing situations without undergoing any major structural changes. The most important factor that has acted to the dynamics of the family is economic in nature which is the crux of the retiree's problem.

Avoidance of or not having economic dependence on children, and democratic approach to the management of family have been found characteristic of the retirees in Tirupati. The same is said to be true of the retirees residing in other urban centers in India (Desai and Naik 1970: 65,97).

A majority of the retirees show an increased need for religious experience and also an overwhelming proportion continue their pre-retirement religious interests even after their retirement. Commitment to religion is more serious among a few who spend more time in religious practices. Dependence on children for financial support to fulfil some religious activities created disappointment among the retirees and the pursuit of leisure time activity with the help of family members sometime become hard. This finding is broadly in conformity with Obrach's finding which states that "Most people carry on the religious beliefs and habits formed earlier in life (Orbach 1961:530-540). Those retirees whose interest has increased in religion have two reasons to mention. One is that they developed interest in religion in later years i.e., after attaining 55 years of age. The other is that they have equated their achievements with religion. More than 17 percent of the retirees have shown a decrease in their interest in religion which can be attributed on understanding the fact that the non-religious people are neither punished nor rewarded for being non-religious.

Retirees utilized some of their leisure time in the worshipping of God. More number of the gazetted than the non-gazetted retirees spend their time in attending clubs and more number of the gazetted than the non-gazetted joined various associations to spend time.

Many gazetted retirees did not feel that they are isolated from others after retirement whereas slightly more than one-third of the non-gazetted feel that they are isolated from others. This is suggestive of financial and psychological independence of the retired non-gazetted employees while it is apparent that more non-gazetted retirees would have liked closer rapport with others. While investigating into the leisure-time activities of the aged in an Indian town Menachery says that the respondents have more than one way of filling in their long hours of leisure (Menachery 1987:126). Likewise the finding on leisure-time activities of the retirees in Tirupati speaks about the multitudinal activities of the aged in utilizing their leisure-time.

Majority of the gazetted and non-gazetted retirees have pressed their opinion that they lack companionship on account of losing a friend. This is because in old age friends of their age give good emotional support. Losing children is also an important cause of lack of companionship. Gazetted and non-gazetted retirees do no9t show differential patterns in this respect proving that these are status free factors that show up in old age.

Nearly half the number of retirees agreed that there is a change in relations with their children along with their age. This is suggestive of the problems due to generation gap. It is also apparent that the gazetted retirees did not bother about their children making important decisions while the non-gazetted retirees felt less secure and wanted to have a say in the family matters thereby proving their importance.

Authoritarian attitudės and approaches are out-moded and a significant number of the retirees changing to this way of dealing with things shows nothing but their problematic approach which brings them conflicts in the times to come.

Employees mostly in their post-retirement life become more and more susceptible to chronic diseases, physical disabilities and mental incapacities. Many of the ailments and diseases remain relatively within the tolerance capacity of the adults and they pull on with them without experiencing serious handicaps in the day-to-day activities. But, with decreased body strength and increased mental worries and economic strains, the individuals ultimately submit to them in old age. The aged men are found to complain about sudden deterioration in their health. Mental troubles including depression, anxiety and obsession are found to be common to both the gazetted and the non-gazetted retirees. Worrying about problems of health is more frequent among the relatively poor respondents on account of their inability to get adequate medicines and nutritive diet.

Some of the health problems of the aged respondents can be attributed to social values. The idea that old age is an age of ailments and physical infirmities is deeply rooted in the respondents' mind and many of the sufferings and physical troubles within the curable limits are accepted as natural and inevitable by the aged. Some of the adjustment problems associated with certain rolesets of the aged arise primarily due to their physical conditions and health factors. Diseases like arthritis, heart troubles and vision troubles have not only curtailed physical movements but also made their social interaction difficult. Moreover, such physical handicaps necessitated great dependence on others. Good health and a disease-free body or at least diseases that do not curtail a person's movements and interactions are quite important in satisfactory social adjustment during old age also. Physical well-being and health in old age also depend considerably on the life-long habits and ways of living of the people.

Anderson rightly points out that "Our bodies need simple, wholesome foods to build and maintain the highest peak of efficiency. We must learn to make the right choice, not only during the older years but all throughout the life. Sensible habits of living will mean far more than any pill or tonic regardless of how highly advertised it may be." (Anderson 1961:33). These comments will help the retire overcome their health problems at least to a certain extent.

Equally important in this context is the understanding of aging as a social problem. The following comments are appropriate in this regard.

Kuhn's observations are relevant in the study of aging. "Recognition of aging as a social problem is recent, recognition of aging as a social scientific problems is more recent still. The social scientific study of aging needs, but currently lacks, widely shared paradigms that would provide common conceptualization of issues, standard measurements, and clearly defined agendas for the systematic testing of hypotheses derived from theory. Applied, problem-orientated studies of the societal consequences of aging predominate; but increasingly sophisticated theory and research techniques are not available to social scientists for use in describing, monitoring, and forecasting social issues posed by an aging population. No single theoretical perspective organizes substantive research on the social aspects of aging. In fact, methodological issues have dominated the attention of social scientists in recent years." (Kuhn 1970).

The disengagement thesis has generated a lot of discussion about the adequacy as a theoretical model for explaining adjustment in old age. Disengagement theory proposed to explain subjective well-being and identified the casual mechanism as fundamentally intrinsic and hence inevitable psychological age-related processes

(Maddox and Campbell 1985:6). The thesis has been put under critical review by its opponents as well as by others. George Maddox observes that the "empirical evidence in support of disengagement as modal, has not convinced even its advocates." He points out two theoretical objections to the hypotheses generated by the disengagement formation, for example, is its tendency to treat as relatively insignificant those variations in the constraints of social environment and in the cumulative patterns of experiences which constitute biographies of individuals (Maddox 1966:130).

Considering the above theories it is understood that neither the disengagement approach nor the activity approach is clear to be the basic or fundamental approach. But successful aging in old age is a matter of a dynamic relationship between the aged and his social environment. The adjustment could be successful only when both the individual and his social environment fulfil mutual expectations and responsibilities. The adjustment pattern has necessarily to undergo change with the passage of time in old age also.

The following conclusions may be made out of the results obtained, at the theoretical or abstract level.

Hierarchy of problems and the differentials of problems have a direct correspondence with the pre-retirement status of the respondents. This status is financial, personal as well as social which decides the hierarchy or the variety of problems. This status again decides the post-retirement socio-cultural participation of the retirees. The literary status of the retirees has a direct bearing upon the socio-psychological factors in the post-retirement period.

Post-retirement insecurity has a direct link with the fact whether a person bequeaths away his property to his children or not, the self–conscious and the self-esteem of the retirees is based upon several factors that exist and condition in the post-retirement period.

Social traditions and customs compel the retirees to carry their separate indentity into their daily routine. The youth again call them to cope with the changing values, new styles of living and aggressive challenges of the outside world to establish their authority in the society. This is a testimony to the fact that tradition and modernity go hand in hand conflicting one another. A sort of peaceful coexistence between culturally two opposite phenomena is apparent.

Certain social, economic and health problems are not based on status dichotomy. This conceptualization permits a comprehensive approach to a condition that far transcends official status discriminations.

The financial crisis among the retirees is a result of the fact that these pensioners belong to a fixed income group and do not keep pace with the other parts of the society whose economic position is often revised. So the financial status of the retirees has a direct bearing upon the Governments' policy matters. On the whole the respondents are protected by their family members, relatives and in some cases a few neighbours. These retirees are definitely on a broad scale better off than their counterparts in the West. So, family remains as the best resort to people in their post-retirement life which will be sustained if an effective national policy to ameliorate the economic conditions of the retirees from time to time is to be drafted and surveillance of the policy implementation is to be facilitated.

Many retirees who are energetic can be made to participate in community development works and social work in and around the places. In the light of Jawahar Rozgar Yojana (Jawahar Employment Scheme) this can be made practical thereby helping the retirees to meet their financial needs.

Planners, policy-makers, administrators and social gerontologists have also now identified thorough investigation into the economic, social, physical and psychological conditions of the gazetted and non-gazetted retirees as a top priority area of research.

A great deal of light has been thrown on the life and problems of the retirees which can be critically evaluated for a sustained national perspective plan to meet and better the socio-economic, socio-psychological and medical needs of the aged in general and retirees in particular in India.

APPENDIX I

Checklist of the Aspects of Retirement Covered By the Research Conducted in India and Other Countries. Those pertaining to India are marked by an Asterisk

Sl. No.	Broad aspect of Retirement covered by the researches	Studies on Specific Aspect
1	2	3
1.	Pre-retirement conditins	1. Institutionalization of retirement
		i. Arguments for and against fixing an age for retirement.
		ii. Criterion for accepting a particular age for retirement.
		iii. Attitude of persons with different occupational levels towards retirement age.
		iv. Attitudinal changes over the years towards retirement age.
		2. Factors behind retirement:
		i. Societal changes.
		ii. Changing demographic structure

Sl. No.	Broad aspect of Retirement covered by the researches	Studies on Specific Aspect
1	2	3
		iii. Women's participation in the labour force.
		iv. Changing pattern of state economy.
		v. Rationalization and bureaucratization of industrial sector.
		vi. The working-man complex.
		vii. Retirement policies
		viii. Changes in family structure.
		ix. Cultural values.
2.	Pre-retirement conditions	1. Psychological changes
		i. Feelings of frustration
		ii. Prevalence of mental disorder in elderly retirees.
		iii. Sense of alienation in the aged.
		2. Dynamics of adjustment
		i. Healthy adjustment
		ii. Maladjustment
		iii. Dynamics of adjustment
		iv. Religion and religious factors helping adjustment.

Sl. No.	Broad aspect of Retirement covered by the researches	Studies on Specific Aspect
1	2	3
		v. Adjustment to institutional setting. vi. Role of activity level and engagement in adjustment vii. Heterogeneity of post-retirement adjustment. viii. Sex differences in adjustment ix. Patterns of adjustment. 3. Morale dimensions i. Life-satisfaction ii. Degree of morale iii. Morale dimensions namely depression, irritability and will to live. 4. Attitudes i. Toward retirement before retirement. ii. Determination of favourable attitudes toward retirement. iii. Toward death iv. Society's attitudes toward old age, retirement and aging process.

Sl. No.	Broad aspect of Retirement covered by the researches	Studies on Specific Aspect
1	2	3
		v. Retirees attitudes toward specific events and aspects.
		5. Health
		i. Physical state of recent retirees
		ii. Mortality rate as an indicator of the health of the retirees.
		6. Family and Social relationships
		i. Family composition
		ii. Patterns of interaction
		iii. Role of the retirees in the family
		iv. Dwelling patterns of the retirees.
		v. Loss of social status of the retirees in the family.
		7. Work and activity
		i. Levels of pre-retirement work and activity even after retirement.
		ii. Nature of occupations and time of retirement.
		iii. Meaning of work for different categories of workers.

Sl. No.	Broad aspect of Retirement covered by the researches	Studies on Specific Aspect
1	2	3
		iv. Relation between continued activity and life satisfaction
		v. Choices between continued employment or immediate retirement.
		vi. Type of activity preferred after retirement
3.	Pre-retirement problems	1. General problems
		i. Psycho-socio changes
		ii. Economic changes
		iii. Physical and physiological
		iv. Separation via divorce or death
		v. Bereavement problems
		vi. Change of locality as a result of retirement when the individual is not prepared for it.
		vii. Pre-occupations over the imminent loss of work
		2. Psychological problems
		i. Retirement as a source of anxiety
		ii. Deterioration in the performance level

Sl. No.	Broad aspect of Retirement covered by the researches	Studies on Specific Aspect
1	2	3
		iii. Deduction in feelings of confidence and personal worth.
		iv. Dependency problem such as subordinate function in the family and Society.
		v. Dissatisfaction with oneself, negative attitudes and depression, strong inferiority complex.
		vi. Impending death as a preoccupation of the retired.
		3. Economic problems
		i. Income problem
		ii. Changing rules of social security.
		iii. Inflation, rising cost of living and reduction in the income of retirees.
		4. Housing problems
		i. Physical need for housing the retirees
		ii. Psychological impact of housing arrangements.
		iii. Sociological problems arising out of retirement communities.

Sl. No.	Broad aspect of Retirement covered by the researches	Studies on Specific Aspect
1	2	3
		iv. Theoretical basis of retirement communities.
		v. Models of new communities
		vi. Emotional and personal loss on account of bureaucratic structure of nursing homes.
		vii. Approach towards retirement homes.
		viii. Retirement, migration and permanent settlement.
		ix. Relationship between attitudes toward housing arrangements and adjustment of the individuals.
		5. Personality problems
		i. Personality factors in relation to problems & difficulties of the retirees.
		ii. Types of personalities and types of problems of the retirees.
		6. Problems of women retirees
		i) Sex differences in the problems of retirement
		ii. Combined effects of being female and old.

Sl. No.	Broad aspect of Retirement covered by the researches	Studies on Specific Aspect
1	2	3
		iii. Mental health status of women retirees.
		7. Problems of retired migrants
		i. Retired migrants and their specific problems
		ii. Clash of cultures of the resident retired and retired migrant
		8. Societal attitudes as creators of problems
		i. Societal attitudes towards retirement in specific cultures
		ii. Stereotyping behaviour & physical symptoms to aging per Sec.
4.	Studies on the future of retirees	1. Age of retirement
		i. Arguments for and against fixing an age for retirement
		ii. Criteria for accepting a particular age for retirement
		iii. Attitudes of persons with different occupational levels towards retirement age.
		iv. Attitudinal changes over the years towards

Sl. No.	Broad aspect of Retirement covered by the researches	Studies on Specific Aspect
1	2	3
		retirement age.
		2. Planning & preparations for retirement
		i. Need for preparing a person for a smooth transition from work life to a period of retirement or reduced work life.
		ii. Counselling problems in retirement assistance.
		iii. Attitudinal changes as a result of pre-retirement planning programme
		iv. Adult education programme participation and ease of participation
		v. Communication network with the retirees
		vi. Pre-retirement counseling

APPENDIX II

The families of the aged respondents are classified according to the criteria given by Murdock (1949) in his book "Social Structure"(1-23).

S.No.	Types of family	Definitions
1	2	3
1.	Nuclear family	"It consists typically of a married man and woman with their offspring, although in individual cases one or more additional persons may reside with them"(Murdock 1949:1) Following the definition of nuclear family given by Murdock, the present study has classified the nuclear families among the aged as shown below: **i. complete nuclear family** It consists of a man, his wife and his child or children who may be own or adopted. **ii. Complete nuclear family with dependents** It consists of a man, his wife and his child or children who may be own or adopted and unmarried or widowed sister, widowed father or mother or physically disabled

S.No.	Types of family	Definitions
1	2	3
		brother or husband. **iii. Incomplete nuclear family** If a nuclear family consists of a young married couple or aged couple if a domestic group consists of father and children or mother and children it may be called an incomplete nuclear family. **iv. Incomplete nuclear family with dependents** If an incomplete nuclear family consists of one or more dependents, who may be the unmarried or widowed sister, widowed father or mother or physically disabled brother of husband, it may be called an incomplete nuclear family with dependents.
2.	Extended family	"The extended family includes two or more nuclear families united by consanguineal kinship such as those between parent and child or between two siblings" (Murdock 1949:23). Following the definition of an extended family given by Murdock the present study has classified the extended families into sub-types as explained below: **i. Complete vertically extended family** It consists of a man, his wife, his married son, his daughter-in-law and his sons' children.

S.No.	Types of family	Definitions
1	2	3
		ii. Complete vertically extended family with dependents If the complete vertically extended family contains one or more dependent such as widowed sister, disabled brother and unmarried, widowed or divorced daughter, it may be called a complete vertically extended family with dependents. **iii. Complete horizontally extended family** It consists of married brothers, their spouses and their children. **iv. Complete horizontally extended family with dependents** If the complete horizontally extended family includes a dependent such as widowed sister, disabled brother and unmarried, widowed or divorced daughter. **v. Incomplete vertically extended family** It consists of a couple, their married son, their daughters-in-law. **vi. Incomplete horizontally extended family** It consists of only married brothers and their spouses.

SOURCE : Murdock, 1949: Social Structure, New York: The Macmillan Company (pages1-23).

References

1. Agruso, Victor M. Learning in the later years – principles educational gerontology. New York: Academic press, 1978.

2. Aldrich, C. and Mendhoff E. Relocation of the aged and disabled: a mortality study. Journal of American Geriatrics Society, 1983, 11, 401-408.

3. Anand, Santosh S. Belongingness and mental health: some research findings. Acta psychologica, 1967, 27, 391-396.

4. Anantaraman, R.N. Adjustment and its correlates in old age. Indian Journal of Clinical Psychology, 1979, 6, 165-168.

5. ——————Physical health and adjustment in old age. Journal of Psychological Researches, 1981, 25, 46-50.

6. —————— Perception and Stereotypes toward old age by two generations. Journal of Psychological Researches, 1984, 28, 170-173.

7. Anderson, Nels. Work and Leisure. London: Routledge and Degan Paul, 1961, 33.

8. Asnes, Daniel P. and Shulman, Helen. Florid Psychosis after retirement in a 68 year old man - a case study report. Journal of Geriatric Psychiatry, 1976, 6, 237-253.

9. Atchley, Robert C. Retirement as social institution. Annual Review of Sociology, 1982, 8, 266-287.

10. Bacharach, Samuel B. and Aichen, Michael. The impact of alienation, meaninglessness, and meritocracy on supervision and subordinate satisfaction. Social Forces, 1979, 57, 853-870.

11. Balles, Paul B., Reese, Hayne W. and Lipsitt, Lewis P. Life-span developmental psychology. Annual Review of Psychology, 1980, 31, 69.

12. Banerjee, Saradendu. Problems of old age: Psychoanalytic perspective. Samiksa, 1983, 37, 3-14.

13. Barkar, Lewellys F. Physical changes in old age and their effects upon mental attitudes. In George Lawton. New goals for old age. New York: Columbia University, 1951.

14. Barron, Milton L., Streib, Gordon, and Suchman, E.A. Research on the social disorganization of retirement. American Sociological Review, 1952, 17, 479-482.

15. Barron, Milton L. The Aging American: An Introduction to Social Gerontology and Geriatrics. New York: Thomas Y. Crowell Company, 1961.

16. Bartus, Raymond T., Dean, Reginald, L. Beer, Bernard and Lippa, Arnold S. The cholinergic hypothesis of geriatric memory dysfunction. Science, 1982, 217, 408-417.

17. Baum, Steven K. and Boxley, Russell L. Depression and age identification. Journal of Clinical Psychology, 1983, 39, 584-590.

18. Berger, Dale, Young, Jeffry and Heebner. Aging in the Inland Empire: a need assessment survey of older persons in Sun Bernardino country, California. Catalog of Selected Documentation in Psychology, 1982, 12, 31-32.

19. Berghorn, Forrest J. The urban elderly – a study of life satisfaction. New Jeresy: Allenheld and Osmun, 1978.

20. Bernard, Harold W. Towards better personal adjustment. New York: McGraw-Hill Book Company, 1951.

21. Bhattacharjee, P.J. Population growth and socio-economic development of India. The Journal of Family Welfare, 1982, 28, 41-48.

22. Bhatia, H.S. "Aging and Society: A Sociological Study of Retired Public Servants", Udaipur, 1983, Arya's Book Centre Publishers.

23. Bharat Pensioners' Samaj, Problems of Pensioners in Jabalpur. Jabalpur: Jabalpur Branch of Bharat Pensioners' Samaj, 1971.

24. Bhojaraj, Shewak. Mental health through recreation. Indian Journal of Social Work, 1964, 9, 2-3.

25. Biren, James E. (ed). Handbook of aging and the individual. Chicago: The University of Chicago press, 1961.

26. Blanker, Margaret. Cultural Values and Dependency in Later Life. In R.A. Dalish (ed). The Dependencies of old people, Occasional Papers in Gerontology No.6 Institute of Gerontology, University of Michigan - Wayne State university, 1969.

27. Blum, Stephen R. and Minkler, Meredith. Toward a continuum of caring alternative: community based care for the elderly. Journal of Social Issues, 198, 15 - 133-152.

28. Borsay, Peggy L. Anderson. Information sources and interpersonal influences during transition to retirement: A study among state university retirees. Ohio: The Ohio State University, 1976.

29. Bose, Ashish, Aspects of aging in India. Social Action, 1982, 32, 1-29.

30. Brink, T.L. The battle against senility. Mental Health, 1977, 61, 10-11.

31. Bromley, D.B. The psychology of human aging. Middlesex: Penguin Books, 1966.

32. Brown, Robert G. Family structure and social isolation of older persons. In Erdman Palmore. (ed) Normal aging. Durham N.C., Duke University Press, 1970.

33. Buhler, Charlette, Keith-spiegel, and Thomas, Karla. Developmental Psychology. In Benjamin B. Wolman. Handbook of general psychology. New Jersey: Prentice-Hall, 1973.

34. Busse, E.W. Psychoneurotic reactions and defence mechanisms in the aged. In P.H. Hoch and J. Jubin (eds). Psychopathology of aging. New York: Grune and Stratton, 1961.

35. Butler, Robert N. Ageism: A foreward. Journal of Social Issues, 1980, 36, 8-11.

36. Bynum, Jack E., Cooper, B.L. and Acuff, F. Gene. Retirement reorientation: Senior adult education. Journal of Gerontology, 1987, 33, 253-261.

37. Carp C.M., Person situation congruence in engagement. Gerontologist, 1968, 8, 184-188.

38. Caron, Ruth Shonle et al. Personal adjustment in old age. Chicago: Science Research Associates, 1949.

39. Chappel, Neena L. and Havens, Betty. Old and Female: Testing the double jeopardy hypothesis. The Sociological Quarterly, 1980, 21, 157-171.

40. Chaudury, Rafigul Huda. The aged in Bangladesh. Social Action, 1982, 32, 20-38.

41. Chavan, Albert and Fischer, Lucy Rose. Retirement and inter-state migration. Social Forces, 1979, 57, 1365-1380.

42. Chown, Shelia M. Human ageing. Middlesex: Penguins, 1977.

43. Clark, Margaret and Barbara Anderson, G. Culture and aging: An anthropological study of older Americans. Springfield Ills: Charles C. Thomas, 1967.

44. Covalt, N.K. The Meaning of Religion to Old People. In C.B. Veddar and A. S. Lefkowitz (eds). Problems of the Aged. Springfield, III, Charles C. Thomas. 1965, 215-224.

45. Cumming, E., Dean, L.R., Neweli, D.S. and McCaffrey, I. Disengagement: a tentative theory of aging. Sociometry, 1960, 23, 23-25.

46. Dayal, N.V. Madgaonkar, J.S. and Dhasandriah, A.S. Study of adjustment of aged men and women to their day to day activities. Paper presented in the National Seminar on psychological aspects of the elderly. Tirupati, June, 1983.

47. Deo, Pratibha and Bhullar, Jatinder. Relationship of physical efficiency to self concept, intelligence and achievement. Psychological Studies. 1974, 19, 56-59.

48. Deoras, Usha and Janabandhu, D.S. Adjustment in old age: an introductory survey, 1979.

49. Desai, K.G. and Naik, R.D. Problems of Retired People in Greater Bombay. Bombay: Tata Institute of Social Sciences, 1970.

50. Eden, Dov and Jacoboson, Dan. Propensity to retirement among elder executives. Journal of Vocational Behaviour,

1979, 8, 145-154.

51. Eisderfer, Carl and Lawton, M. Powell. The psychology of adult development and aging. Washington: American Psychological Association, 1973.

52. Ekerdt, David, J, Rose, Charles L., Bosse, Raymond and Costa, Paul. Longitudinal change in preferred age of retorememt. Journal of Occupational Psychology, 1976, 49, 161-169.

53. Entine, Alan D. Counselling for mid-life and beyond. Vocational Guidance Quarterly, 1977, 25, 332-336.

54. Eran, Mordechai and Jacobson, Dan. Expectancy theory prediction of the preference to remain employed or to retire. Journal of Gerontology, 1976, 31, 605-610.

55. Fox, Jodith Haff Women, Work and retirement. Dissertation Abstract International, 1976, 37, 1237.

56. Fox, Judith H. Effects of retirement and former work life on women's adaptation in old age. Journal of Gerontology, 1977, 32, 192-202.

57. Friedman, E.A. and Havighurst. R.J. The meaning of work and retirement. Chicago: The University of Chicago Press, 1954.

58. Fuller, Robert L. and Redfering. David L. Effects of pre-retirement planning on the retirement adjustment of military personnel. Sociology of work and occupations, 1976, 479-487.

59. Geist, Harold. The psychological aspects of the aging process with sociological implications. Missouri: Warren M. Green Ind., 1968.

60. Geriatric Focus Report, 1966, 5, 9, 4-5.

61. Gillin, J.L. Dittmer, C.E., Colbert, Roy J. and Kastler, N.M. Social Problems. Bombay: The Times of India Press, 1965.

62. Goldfarb, A.I. 'Dependencies of old age'. In R.A. Dalish (ed.) Dependencies of Old People. Occasional Papers on Gerontology No.6, Institute of Gerontology, University of Michigan – Wayne State University. 1969, 2.

63. Goode, William J. Principles of Sociology. New Delhi. Tata

McGraw-Hill Publishing Com. Ltd., 1977.

64. Goudy, Willis J., Powers, Edward and Keith, Patricia. The work satisfaction, retirement – attitude typology: profile examination. Experimental Aging Research, 1975, 1, 267-279.

65. Graebner, William. A history of retirement: The meaning and function of an American institution 1885-1978. New Haven: Yale University Press, 1978.

66. Graebner, W. A History of Retirement. The Meanings and Function of an American Institution. New Haven: Yale University Press, 1980.

67. Green, B., Parham I.A. Kleff, R. and Plisuk, Merc. Introduction. Journal of Social Issues, 1980, 36, 1-7.

68. Gubrium, Jaber F. Time, role and self in old age. New York: Human Science Press, 1976.

69. Gurland, Barry, Reevaluating the place of evaluation in planning for alternatives of institutional care for the elderly. Journal of Social Issues, 1981, 37, 51-69.

70. Hall, G.S: Senescence, The Last Half of Life. New York: Appleton and Company, 1922.

71. Hamlin, R.M.A. Utility theory of old age. Gerontologist, 1967, 7, 37-45.

72. Hampe, Gray D. and Blevins, Audie D. Primary group interaction of residents in a retirement hotel. International Journal of Aging and Human development, 1975, 6, 309-320.

73. Hardikar and Bhatia . Old age –a medical and social review in S. N. Gajendragadkar. Disabled in India. Bombay: Somaiya Publications 1983.

74. Havighurst, R. J. and R. Albereht, Older People New York : Longmans, 1953.

75. Havighurst, R. J. Successful aging. In R. J. Willliams, C. Tibbitts and W. Donahue (eds) Process of aging New York: Atherton Press, 1963.

76. Havighurst, R. J. 1973. Social roles, work, leisure, and education. In Carl Eisodorfer and M. Powell Lawton (eds), The Psychology of Adult Development and Aging. Washington:

D. C. American Psychological Association, 1973.

77. Haynes, Suzanne, G., McMichael, Anthony J., and Tyroler, H. A. The relationship of normal, involuntary retirement to early mortality among U.S. Rubber workers. Social Science and Medicine, 1977, 11, 105-114.

78. Hayslip, Bert and Panek, Paul E. Physical self-maintenance, mental status, and personality, in institutionalized elderly adults. Journal of Clinical Psychology, 1983, 39, 479-485.

79. Heron, Alastair and Chown, Sheila M. Expectations of supervisors concerning older workers. In R. A. Williams, C. Tibbitts and W. Donahue. Process of aging , Vol. 1. New York: Atherton Press, 1970.

80. Heyman, D.K. and Jeffers, Francis. The influence of race and socio-economic status upon the activities and attitudes of the aged. In Erdman Palmore. (ed) Normal aging, Durham, N. C. Duke University Press, 1970.

81. Hunter, Wooddraw W. A retirement reader's check-list. Michigan: University of Michigan, 1975.

82. Hurlock, E.B. Developmental psychology (3rd ed.). New Delhi: Tata McGraw-Hill, 1968, 854.

83. Hyden, Sven, Workers' and employers' attitudes toward retirement age and pensions. In Richard H. Williams, Clark Tibbitts and Wilma Donahue. (eds) Process of aging. New York: Atherton Press, 1963.

84. Jamuna D. and Ramamurthi, P. Age adjustment and husband wife communication of middle aged and older women. Journal of Psychological Researches, 1984, 31, 145-218.

85. Jaslow, Philip, Employment, retirement and morale among older women, Journal of Gerontology, 1976, 31, 212-218.

86. Jeffers, F.C., Nichols, C.R. and Eisdorfer, D. Attitude of the older persons towards death. In Erman B. Palmore. Normal Aging. Durham N.C: Duke University Press, 1970.

87. Jonas, Karen, Women and work: An analysis of attitudes towards work of elderly residents of public housing. Wisconsin Sociologists, 1976, 13, 20-30.

88. Joshi, C.K. Medical problems of old age. Indian Journal of Gerontology, 1971, 3, 64-68.

89. Kalish, Richard A. and Moriwak, Sharon, The World of the elderly Asian American. Journal of Social Issues, 1973, 29, 187-209.

90. Kapadia, R. L. Pensioners, Society and state. Address to the Marathwada Retired Person's Association, Aurangabad, 1977.

91. Kaplan, O. J. (Ed), Mental Disorders in Later Life, Stanford University Press, Stanford, 1945.

92. Kerchoff, Alan C. Husband-wife expectations and reactions to retirement. In Sheila. M. Chown. Human aging. Middlesex: Penguins, 1972.

93. Kastenbaum, Robert and Costa, Paul T. Psychological perspectives of death. Annual Review of Psychology, 1977, 28, 225-249.

94. Keily, Margaret C. and Dudek, Stephaiane Z. Attitudes towards death in aged persons. Psychiatric Journal of the University of Ottawa, 1977, 2, 181-184.

95. Kelkar, Vasundhara. A psychological study of the problem of old age adjustment. Unpublished dissertation for M.A. Poona: Poona University, 1974.

96. Kikuchi, Takekatsu, Sei, Toshio and Ooe, Atsushi. Socialization after adulthood: a social psychological study on the retirement process of old males in a fishing village in North East Japan. Johuku Psychologica Tolia, 1975, 34, 132-143.

97. Kleemeier, R.W. (ed) Aging and Leisure. New York: Oxford University Press, 1961.

98. Kogan, N. and Wallagh, M.A. Age changes in values and attitudes. J. Gerontology, 1961, 16, 272-280.

99. Kreps, Janunita M. (Ed.) Employment, Income and Retirement Problems of the Aged, Duke University Press, Durham, North Carolina, 1963.

100. Kuhn, T.S. The Structure of Scientific Revolutions, 1970, 4. 2nd Ed., Chicago. University of Chicago Press. In Handbook

of Aging and the Social Sciences 2nd ed. by Robert H. Binstock and Ethel Shanas, New York; Van Nostrand Reinhold Company Inc., 1985.

101. Kreps, J.M. Employment Policy and Income Maintenance for the Aged. In John C. McKinney and Frank T. de Vyver (eds.). Aging and Social Policy. New York: Appleton – Century Crafts. 1966, 136.

102. Kuhlen, Raymond G. Aging and Life adjustment. In James Birren (ed.), Handbook of aging and the individual Chicago: The University of Chicago Press, 1959.

103. Langer, E. and Abelson, R.A. Patient by any other name. Journal of Consulting and Clinical Psychology, 1974, 42, 4-9.

104. LeCourse, Wilfred and Roy, Jean. Violence and the marginalization of the elderly in today's society. Canada's Mental Health, 1982, 30, 25-35.

105. Lee, Gray R. Residential location and fear of crime among the elderly. Rural Sociology, 1982, 47, 655-669.

106. Lowenthal, Marjorie Fiske and Boler, Deetje, Voluntary versus involuntary social withdrawal. In Shiela M. Chown. Human aging, Middlesex. Penguins, 1972.

107. Lownethal, M.F. and Haven C. Interaction and adaptation: intimacy as a critical variable. American Sociological Review, 1960, 25, 385-394.

108. Lundberg, G.A. et al. Leisure: A sub-urban study quoted in Nels Anderson, 1943, 33.

109. Maddox. Activity and Morale - a longitudinal study of selected elderly subjects. Social Forces, 1965, 2, 195-204.

110. Maddox, G.L. Retirement as a social event in the United States, in John C. Mckinney and Frank T. de Vyver, (eds.) Aging and Social Policy. New York; Appleton-Century Crofts. 1966, 130.

111. Maddox, G.L. and Campbell, R.T. Handbook of Aging and The Social Science (eds.), Robert H. Binstock and Ethel Shanas. New York: Van Nostrand Reinhold Company Inc. 1985, 6.

112. Mahajan, A. Problems of the Aged in Unorganised Sector. Delhi: K.M. Mittal Publications, 1987.

113. Malik, P.L. The Industrial Law, Lucknow: Eastern Book Company, 1980.

114. Mamoria, C.B. Principals of social security. Allahabad: Kitab Mahal Service Ltd.,1965.

115. Martin, William C., Bengtson, Vern L., Ackock, Alan C. Alientation and age: a contest specific approach. Social Forces, 1974, 53, 165-274.

116. Marulasiddaiah, H.M. Old people of Makunti, Dharwar: Karnataka University, 1972.

117. McConnell, James V. Understanding Human Behaviour. New York: Hold, Rinehart and Winston, 1977.

118. Menachery, George. Retirement in India: A psycho-social study. Nidadavole: Vianney Publication, 1987.

119. Meyer, Sheldon L. Andragogy and the aging adult learner. Educational Gerontology, 1977, 2, 115-122.

120. Miles, W.R. "Age and Human Ability" Psychological Review, Vol.40: 90-123. 1933.

121. Ministry of Health and Welfare. Survey on the actual conditions of the people Tokyo: Ministry of Health and Welfare, 1973.

122. Ministry of Health and Welfare, KOSEI HAKUSHO. Health and Welfare White Paper (Government Printing Office, Ministry of Finance), Tokyo: 1974.

123. Moberg. David O. The Christian religion and personal adjustment in old age. American Sociological Review.1953, 18, 87-90.

124. Moos Rudold H. Specialised living environments for older purpose: a conceptual framework for evaluation. Journal of Social Problems, 1982, 30, 40-50.

125. Mukherjee, M. and Upadhyay, S.N. adjustment, anxiety and health. Indian Psychological Review. 1980, 19, 11-13.

126. Munjal, engagement theory and successful aging. Paper

presented at 5th All India Convention of Clinical Psychologists. New Delhi, 1974.

127. Murdock, G.P.Social Structure. New York: The Macmillan Company, 1949.

128. Nayar, P.K.B. A Study of the working of old age pension schemes in Kerala. Trivandrum: University of Kerala, 1980.

129. Nair, T. Krishnan. Older people in rural Tamil Nadu. Madras: Madras School of Social Work (Mimeo).

130. Orbach, Harold L. Normative aspects of retirement, in Clark Tibbitts and Wilma Donahue (eds) Social and Psychological aspects of aging, New York: Columbia University Press, 1968.

131. ———————— Social values and the institutionalization of retirement. In Richard H. Williams, Clark Tibbitts and Wilma Dobahue. (eds), Process of aging. Vol. II, New York: Atherton Press, 1973.

132. Padmanabha. Population of India - some dimensions. Yojana, 1983, 27, 4-6.

133. Paintal, Harinder Kaur. Some factors related to successful aging in medical men. Indian Journal of Clinical Psychology, 1979, 6, 27-33.

134. ————Engagement theory and successful aging. Indian Journal of Clinical Psychology, 1976, 3, 101-109.

135. Palmore, E.B. Physical, mental and social factors in predicting longevity. Gerontologist, 1969, 9, 103-108.

136. Palmore, Erdman, (ed) International Handbook on aging: contemporary developments and Research. Westport: Greenwood Press, 1980.

137. Pamina, Nataya Viktorovna. Preparation for retirement as condition for adaptation to the status of pensioner. Satsiologicheskie Iss bedovaniya, 1979, 6, 101-107.

138. Parkes, C.M. Benjamin, B. Fitzgerald R.G. Broken heart: a statistical study of increased mortality among widowers. British Medical Journal, 1969, 1, 740.

139. Pathak, J.D. Our elderly. Bombay: Medical Research Centre, Bombay Hospital Trust, 1978.

140. ———— Geriatrics in India: Some suggestions. In K.G. Desai. Aging in India. Bombay: Tata Institute of Social Sciences, 1982.

141. Phelps, Herold A. and Handerson, David, Contemporary Social Problems. Prentice-Hall Inc., New York, 1952.

142. Pilisuk, Marc and Minkler, Meredith. Supportive networks: Life ties for the elderly. Journal of Social Issues, 1980, 36, 95-116.

143. Pollock, Oth, Report of Social Science Research Council, New York: 1954.

144. Preme, Mahindra, K. International migration in India. 1961-81. Social Action, 1984, 34, 274-285.

145. Prestone, D.F. Traits endorsed by older non-retired and retired subjects. Journal of Gerontology, 1966, 22, 415-420.

146. Pross, M. Age and sex roles: changes in the position of women in society and the potential consequences for aging and the aged. Psychological Abstract, 1979, 61, 13247.

147. Purohit, C.K. and Sharma, R. "A study of aged 60 years and above in a social Profile" Indian Journal of Gerontology, 1972. Vol. 4; 71-83.

148. Quadagno, Jill, S. Career continuity and retirement of men and women physicians: the meaning of disorderly career. Sociology of work and occupations, 1978, 5, 55-74.

149. Radebold, Preparation for aging and help for the aged. The Berlin model, Information for the elderly. Psychological Abstracts, 1977, 57, 8851.

150. Radha, Devi D. and Ravindran, N. Women's work in India. International Social Science Journal, 1983, 35.

151. Ramachandran, V., Menon, Sara M. and Ramamurthi, B. Psychiatric disorders in subjects aged over fifty. Indian Journal of Psychiatry, 1979, 21,193-198.

152. Ramamurthi, P.V. An adjustment inventory for the aged. Indian Journal of Psychology, 1968, 43, 27-29.

153. ———— Adjustment in later maturity. Psychological Studies, 1976, 21, 41-44.

154. ———— Problems of aging in industry. Journal of the Indian Academy of Applied Psychology, 1965, 2, 30-34.

155. ———Problems of older people - an analysis of age trends. Psychological Studies. 1970, 15, 128-130.

156. ———Age work efficiency and retirement. Bombay Psychologist, 1982, 3, 34-36.

157. Rangaswami, K. Stressful live-events and neurosis in old age. Journal of Psychological researches, 1983, 26, 115-119.

158. Rao, Venkoba. Virudhigirnathan, B.S. and Malathi, R. Mental illness in patients aged fifty and over. Indian Journal of Psychiatry, 14, 319-332.

159. Rao, Venkoba and Madhavan T. Geropsychiatric morbidity survey in a semi urban area near Madurai. Indian Journal of Psychiatry, 1982, 24, 258-267.

160. Ratan, Suresh I. Aging outside the body. Science Today, 1983, 17, 52-55.

161. Ranade, S.N. and Ramachandran, P. Women and employment. Bombay: Tata Institute of Social Sciences,1970.

162. Reichard, Susanne, Livson, Florine and Peterson, Paul G. Adjustment to retirement. In Bernice L. Neugarten. Middle Age and aging. Chicago: The University of Chicago press, 1968.

163. Rodin, Judith and Langer, Ellen. Aging labels – the decline of control and the fall of self esteem Journal of Social Issues, 1980, 36, 12-29.

164. Rosow, Irving. Retirement housing and social integration. In Clark Tibbitts and Wilma Donahue (eds). Social and psychological aspects of aging. New York: Columbia University Press, 1962.

165. Rowe, Alan R. Retired academics and research activity. Journal of Gerontology, 1976, 31, 456-461.

166. Ruch, F.L. "Adult learning", Psychological Bulletin, 1933, 30, 387-414.

167. Sati, P.N. Retired people: Their Life-Style and Problems, 1972, Agra: Agra University.

168. Schlenoff, David. Considerations in counselling the retiring career officer for re-employment. Journal of Employment Counselling, 1977, 14, 104-109.

169. Schneiders, A.A. Personality dynamics and mental health. New York: Holt, Rinehart and Winston, 1965.

170. Scott, Frances Gillespie. Factors in the personal adjustment of institutionalized and non-institutionalized aged. American Sociological Review, 1955, 20, 538-546.

171. Seeman, M. On the meaning of alienation. American Sociological Review, 1959, 24, 783-791.

172. Semyonov, Mosha. The social context of women's labor force participation: A comparative analysis. American Journal of Sociology, 1980, 86, 534-550.

173. Shapiro, Vladimir Davydovich and Pyshor, Nicholai, Nesterovich. The social-political activity of pensioners. Sotsiologicheskie Issledovaniya, 1979, 6, 91-98.

174. Sharma, Prayag Raj. Old age in Nepal - some preliminary observations. Social Action, 1982, 32, 39-52.

175. Sharma, K.L.A. Survey of the happiness and unhappiness in old age. Indian Journal of Gerontology, 1971, 3, 76-77.

176. Shaw, Marvin, E. and Wright, Jack, M. Scales for the measurement of attitudes. New York: McGraw-Hill Book Company, 1967.

177. Sheth, Kelaki. Where time stands still. Express magazine Aug.7, 1983.

178. Simpson, I.M. and McKinney, J.C. Social aspects of aging. Durham: Duke University Press, 1966.

179. Singh, Soodan Kirpal. Aging in India. Department of Social Work. Lucknow: University of Lucknow, 1975.

180. Singh, R.B. and Gunthey. The mental health problem of the old age. Indian Journal of Clinical Psychology, 1983, 10, 331-338

181. Sinha, Sunipa. Psychiatric problems of the old age. Samiksha, 1983, 37, 20-25.

182. Sinick, Daniel. New vistas in counseling series: IV Counselling older persons: careers, retirement and dying, New York: Human Science Press, 1977.

183. Slavick, F., Smith, P.C., Shultz, E.B. and Mc-Connell, J.W. Scope. Goals and methodology for the study of retirement policies in the American economy. In Clark Tibbitts and Wilma Donahue. (eds.) Social and psychological aspects of aging. New York: Columbia University Press, 1968.

184. Snow, Robert B. and Havighurst, Robert J. Life-Style types and patterns of retirement of educators. Gerontologist, 1977, 17, 545-552.

185. Soodan, Kirpal Singh. Changing of the aged. Indian Journal of Gerontology, 1972, 4, 50-52.

186. Soodan, Kirpal Singh, 1975. Aging in India, Calcutta, Minerva Associates.

187. Stieglitz, E.J. 'Orientationn in Gerontology' In N.Y. Academy of Medicine, Biological Foundation of Health Education. New York, Columbia. 1950, 96-116.

188. Streib, B. Morale of the retired social problems, 1956, 3, 270-276.

189. Strauss, Harold, Aldrich, Bruce and Lipman, Aaron. Retirement and perceived status loss: an enquiry into some objectives and subjective problems produced by aging. In Jaber F. Gubrium. (ed) Time, role and self in old age. New York: Human Science Press, 1976.

190. Streib B. Morale of the retired. Social problems, 1956, 3, 270-76.

191. Sunelaram, K. Registrar General's population projections, 1981-2001, an appraisal and an alternative approach. Economic and political Weekly, 1984, 19, 1479-1484.

192. Sussman, Marvin B. and Romeis, James C. Family supports for the aged: A comparison of U.S. and Japan Responses. Journal of Comparative Family Studies, 1981, 12, 475-492.

193. Szwarch, M. Activity. Social situation and subjective state of health in old age. The German Journal of Psychology, 1981, 5, 280.

194. Taylor, Shelley, E. Adjustment to treatening events. A theory of cognitive adaptation. American Psychology, 1983, 4, 237-239.

195. Telford, Charles W. and Sawrey, James N. The exceptional individual. New York: Prentice-Hall Ind., 1977.

196. Tibbitts, Clark. First world assembly on aging termed long range success. Aging, 1983, No. 337, 2-5.

197. Tissue, T. Old age and the perception of poverty. Sociology and Social Research, 1972, 53, 331-334.

198. Time 1981, 19th October.

199. Treas, Judith, 1975. 'Aging and the Family'. In Dianna S. Woodruff and James E. Birren (eds). Aging Scientific Perspectives and Social Issues, p.92. New York: D. Van Nostrand.

200. Tuckman, J. and Lorge, I. The best years of life: a study in ranking. Journal of Psychology, 1952, 34, 137-149.

201. Uhlig, Richard H. Employment and retirement of a group of older males. American Sociological Review, 1952, 17, 90-93.

202. Van Santvoort, N.M. Dutch research on older workers and retirement: review. Tijdeschrift voor Gerontologie an Geriatric, 1982, 13, 186-192.

203. Wack, Jeffrey and Rodin, Judith Nursing homes for the aged: The human consequences of legislation shaped environments. Journal of Social Issues, 1978, 34, 6-21.

204. Walker, James W. and Lazer, Harriet. The end of mandatory retirement - implications for management. New York: Wiley, 1978.

205. Walther, Robin J. Economics of Older population in Dianna S. Woodruff and James E. Birren (eds). Aging: Scientific Perspective and Social Issues. New York: D. Van Nostrand . 1975, 340-341.

206. Waters, Elinor and Goodman, Jane. Career counselling for adults, why, when, where and how. Vocational Guidance Quarterly, 1977, 25, 334-343.

207. Weisman, A.D. and Kastenbaum, R. The psychological

autopsy - a study of terminal phases of life. New York: Behaviour Publications, 1968.

208. Williams, Arthur Milton, Recreation for the Aging, Association press, New York, 1953.

209. Wood, Stephan. Managerial reactions to job redundancy through early retirement. The Sociological Review, 1980, 28, 783-807.

210. Woodward, Ann. Housing the elderly, Society, 1982, 19, 52-57.

211. Wright, Hobly, Bennet, Ruth, Simon, Robert and Weinberg, Gladys. Evaluation study of the exploratory visit: an innovative and reach activity of the ILGMU's friendly visiting program. International Journal of Aging and Human Development, 1977-78, 8, 67-82.

212. Zinberg, Norman E. and Kaufman, Irving. Normal psychology of the aging process. New York: International Universities Press. 1963.